'Ruth Ashbee has produced the guide that senior leade
ages to show both why subject-sensitivity matters and
subjects to find intellectual and practical coherence.
through subjects' complex relationships with changing
responsibilities leaders must exercise. Thus, her respect for the truth quests and
traditions of subject communities unlocks bigger educational thinking.'

Christine Counsell, Education Consultant,
Trustee of David Ross Education Trust,
Editor of *Teaching History* journal; formerly History PGCE leader,
University of Cambridge and Director of Education, Inspiration Trust

'Has there ever been an aspect of education more misunderstood, more neglected
and more important than curriculum? For many years the 'curriculum' was broadly
synonymous with the timetable and the subjects a school offered. For teachers, the
job of thinking about what children would study was outsourced to exam boards
and DfE documents. But times they are a-changin'. The past few years has seen
many school leaders and teachers begin to come to terms with the extent of their
ignorance on this most crucial aspect of children's education and there has been
an explosion of interest in curriculum thinking. In the scramble to try to work out
what it means to plan, implement and evaluate a curriculum, there has been a
range of very useful books published but none are quite so coherent and useful as
Ruth Ashbee's. If you read one book on curriculum let it be this one. *Curriculum*
offers an essential handbook for thinking about how the school subjects are organised, what makes each unique and marvellous, and how to induct students into
the wonderful business of making meaning. I have little doubt it will bestride the
narrow educational world like a colossus for many years to come.'

David Didau, Education Writer and Speaker

'The perfect antidote to the tired old generic books that focus on curriculum
because of inspection or accountability, and one that will challenge and demand
that senior leaders do better. Ruth Ashbee has curated a demanding curriculum for
all those – and she makes clear that should be everyone in school leadership – who
have a direct interest in the substance of what pupils learn in school. For teachers
and leaders, this book shows Ashbee to be to curriculum what Lemov is to pedagogy and Willingham is to cognitive science. Brilliant.'

Stuart Lock, CEO, Advantage Schools Trust

Curriculum

Curriculum, or the substance of what is taught, is the core business of schools, and yet little exists in the way of a theory of curriculum for educators. This book sets out the principles of curriculum theory and provides a common framework and practical strategies for the successful implementation and effective management of powerful knowledge-based curriculum for all.

Offering powerful insights across the subject divides, the book explores the key elements of curriculum design including progression, sequencing, substantive and disciplinary knowledge, and the relationships of subjects to their sister disciplines. Providing a crucial foundation for school leadership, it covers:

- curriculum in the contexts of learning, organisational culture and key philosophical and moral ideas

- an explanation of thirteen specialist subjects, with outline mapping of the knowledge

- an emphasis on the cultural elements needed for sustained excellence in curriculum work within schools

- the codification of curriculum and the multiple values of documents for curriculum thinking and execution.

Enabling leaders to analyse and discuss subjects beyond their specialisms, this essential text will equip readers to implement real change by leading intelligently and effectively on curriculum.

Ruth Ashbee is a teacher, senior leader and blogger, and has worked in state comprehensives since qualifying as a teacher of physics in 2005. Specialising in curriculum, teacher development and school improvement, her interests include philosophy, the professionalisation of teaching and the destruction of ivory towers.

Curriculum

Theory, Culture and the Subject Specialisms

Ruth Ashbee

Routledge
Taylor & Francis Group

LONDON AND NEW YORK

First published 2021
by Routledge
2 Park Square, Milton Park, Abingdon, Oxon OX14 4RN

and by Routledge
52 Vanderbilt Avenue, New York, NY 10017

Routledge is an imprint of the Taylor & Francis Group, an informa business

British Library Cataloguing-in-Publication Data
A catalogue record for this book is available from the British Library

Library of Congress Cataloging-in-Publication Data
Names: Ashbee, Ruth (Educator), editor.
Title: Curriculum : theory, culture and the subject specialisms / Ruth Ashbee.
Description: Abingdon, Oxon ; New York, NY : Routledge, 2021. | Includes bibliographical references and index. |
Identifiers: LCCN 2020057622 | ISBN 9780367483753 (hardback) | ISBN 9780367483777 (paperback) | ISBN 9781003039594 (ebook)
Subjects: LCSH: Education–Curricula–Philosophy.
Classification: LCC LB1570 .A787 2021 | DDC 375–dc23
LC record available at https://lccn.loc.gov/2020057622

ISBN: 978-0-367-48375-3 (hbk)
ISBN: 978-0-367-48377-7 (pbk)
ISBN: 978-1-003-03959-4 (ebk)

Typeset in Melior
by SPi Global, India

Contents

1 INTRODUCTION

1.1 The making of meaning

The quest for meaning is as old as humanity itself, and it is our defining feature as humans. Education is both the institution and the process of the sustenance and development of that meaning over the generations. Michael Oakeshott describes this relationship thus:

> As civilized human beings, we are the inheritors [...] of a conversation, begun in the primeval forests and extended and made more articulate in the course of centuries. It is a conversation which goes on both in public and within each of ourselves [...] Education, properly speaking, is an initiation into the skill and partnership of this conversation [...] And it is this conversation which, in the end, gives place and character to every human activity and utterance.[1]

In language, art, religion, music, and mathematics, for thousands of years, we have represented and *lived in* ideas beyond the everyday, the obvious, and the merely adaptive. In science, geography, and history, we seek to understand the world before and beyond us. In sport, we challenge ourselves at the intersection between self, world, and time, and we delight in the moment. In music and art we create beauty and elicit emotion, and when joined with others in our appreciation of these things we find connection. Wherever artefacts from early humans exist, we find evidence of ideas beyond the tangible: images, music, maps, and gods. In sharing this meaning, we are communities. In making meaning, we are conscious.

Over time, our searches for meaning have developed, accumulating more knowledge, becoming increasingly sophisticated, and differentiating, so that today we have a myriad of lenses on the world, each making meaning from different things in different ways. The subject disciplines are the social, cultural, and epistemological structures we have developed over time – to house, treasure, renew, and build this meaning. Through the disciplines we pursue truth, beauty, and ingenuity; we ask and answer questions about the worlds around us and within us; we make new things to express ideas, to be beautiful, and to change the world. It is not just Newton who stood on the shoulders of giants: in studying the subject disciplines we join the towering conversations of humanity, and from these we can all see far.

1.2 The role of schools

School curriculum plays three roles in this story: as a component of democracy, as a renewer of specialists to sustain the disciplines, and as a provider of knowledge for its own sake, for all.

1.2.1 Schools as a component of democracy

Much of the knowledge taught in a school curriculum is directly relevant to participation in democracy, to informed voting, responsible citizenship, critical consumption of media, and accountability of institutions. Beyond this, schools, and in particular departments within schools, must be part of the discourse and policy-making that structure the stewardship of the knowledge in the disciplines. The recontextualisation of knowledge for the school setting – the creation of curriculum in relation to the broader discipline in universities and elsewhere – is core to the ongoing history of human endeavour, and the conversation around this recontextualisation should be ongoing. In this discourse, questions of truth, interpretations, and values are democratised, and a defence against deceit and totalitarianism is offered.[2]

1.2.2 Schools as trainers of future specialists

In teaching students, one of our aims is always that some will pursue the subject or a related specialism, and in this way the disciplines are sustained; they live as practices, their protagonists prepared again and again, throughout the generations. Thus we renew the societal good that comes from the specialised disciplines: from the prosaic, the inventive and the useful, to the beautiful and the cultural, to the meaning that everyone can make from a world in which specialist disciplines exist, and the belonging that develops from that shared yet personal meaning.

1.2.3 Schools as stewards of knowledge for its own sake, for all

Continued study can, of course, only ever be one of our aims, since by definition no student can specialise in everything. We teach the knowledge in the subjects because it is good, because we believe it is worth having. "Knowledge for knowledge's sake", and all the wonder and being-in-the-world that comes with it; this is what schools are for. Whatever paths our students take on leaving school, taking with them the knowledge of the subjects – and the ability to make meaning from the world in the ways crafted in the specialist disciplines – is a wonderful thing, and is the business of schools.

Curriculum, then, is a matter of social and cultural justice. Children spend a limited number of years in school, and a large part of what they leave with is the direct result of the curriculum, of the substance of what has been taught. Our students can leave us with a rich and detailed understanding of the world and our placings in it. They can leave with a sense of ownership and belonging, and the knowledge that knowledge itself is in flux, that it is created in time, and that they themselves may join this story if they wish. They can leave able to join "the great conversations"[3] of humanity, able to participate in the discourse that underpins current affairs, cultural life, and functioning democracy. They can leave with all this, or they can leave with very little. The work of ensuring the former is the work of curriculum leadership.

1.3 The essential tension

As educators become more reflective about the status and role of curriculum, schools and their leaders are increasingly beginning to place curriculum at the heart of what they do, seeking to provide children with ambitious, meaningful, and scholarly knowledge that opens up the worlds of understanding in the disciplines. Any meaningful work on curriculum must necessarily have subject specialism at its heart. Therein lies a paradox: a school needs centralised leadership in order to function, but that leadership must be able to discuss knowledge with the many subject specialisms, many of which will necessarily be outside of subject expertise of school leaders.

How can school leaders effectively lead for curriculum in subjects they know little or nothing about? How can they support the development of their subject leaders and their teams? How can they judge the quality of curriculum work taking place, and identify priorities for development? What questions should they ask subject leaders, both for their own understanding and for the valuable reflection that such conversation can prompt in their interlocutors? This book seeks to answer these questions and provide some structure to the work of curriculum leadership.

1.4 Structure and approach

This book draws together and builds on work from curriculum thinkers, philosophers, and subject specialists, with two key aims. First, it is hoped that the ideas presented here will be useful both to senior leaders (and anyone else interested in curriculum) in leading and developing curriculum work in schools and beyond. The knowledge needed for effective curriculum leadership is diverse and often challenging; to have some of it brought together in one place is, I hope, a worthwhile contribution to the field.

Second, this book is presented as a contribution to a developing discourse around the curriculum in schools. This field is in many ways still in its infancy, and further work is needed in order to establish an agreed professional body of knowledge to sit at the core of our practice in education. Challenges to some of the claims made here are fully anticipated and indeed welcomed, as we forge forward in our quest to illuminate the substance of education, and to build a powerful and enduring theory of curriculum. It is to be hoped that those who continue this curricular conversation will challenge, critique, and probe my assumptions and add to our collective knowledge. As such, the claims here are put forward as contributions and not diktats; this book is an exploration rather than a blueprint.

Following this introduction, in Chapter 2: Curriculum in Context, we explore first the moral arguments for ambitious curriculum, before considering the relations of curriculum to "the knower", in particular how insights from philosophy and cognitive science can provide a theoretical background to our work in curriculum. We then move to the environment and shared understandings needed for effective curriculum work in "A Culture of Curriculum".

In Chapter 3: Curriculum Theory, we make our way through the key components of understanding curriculum, beginning with Bernstein's work on subjects, disciplines, and recontextualisation, establishing clarity over the differences and relations between our school subjects and their cousins in the universities, in industry, and so on. The next section explores sociological and epistemological work on the gazes, quests, truth-statuses and methods for approving knowledge within disciplines in subjects – ideas that are essential in getting at the unique characters of our subject specialisms. In the following section are laid out categories for understanding different types of knowledge within our subjects, and this is followed by an analysis of the relations of knowledge and the implications for curriculum work.

Having made sense of the types of knowledge and the relations of knowledge, we are then able to consider, in the next section, the question of progression, and what it might mean to get better at a particular subject. This is a necessary precursor to our consideration in the following section of sequencing, and the various principles that may apply in the meaningful and effective ordering of material within a curriculum.

In Chapter 4: The Subjects, we visit mathematics, science, geography, history, religious studies, modern foreign languages, art, music, English, physical education, design and technology, food, and computing, attempting to paint a brief picture of their identities and characters, and laying out some key components and features of the knowledge in these subjects, in order to better inform subject-specific curriculum conversations. These analyses explore the ideas laid out in Chapter 3 within the contexts of the subjects, allowing us to use a common language to gain insight into otherwise often opaque areas of specialism.

In Chapter 5: The Codification of Curriculum, we examine the nature and value of codified materials in curriculum work, and explore some examples such as knowledge maps, sequences, models of progression, and booklets, as well as the need to balance the putative permanence of such materials with the need for curriculum to be continuously discussed and developed.

Together these chapters, it is hoped, can provide leaders of curriculum with insight into the structures and workings of curriculum thinking in schools, and begin to offer guidance for the development of this work and the creation of a culture of curriculum as a way of professional life.

1.5 Using this book

1.5.1 The chapters

The chapters in this book are intended to be read in order. In particular, readers seeking to gain insight into the subject specialisms should resist the temptation to rush to Chapter 4 and ensure that, at a minimum, Chapter 3 is read first, since the subject analyses lean heavily on the ideas laid out there. While the chapters deal with fairly diverse areas, each is presented as crucial to effective curriculum work in schools and the interdependence between these areas should not be overlooked. When we speak of developing a culture that treasures the subject specialisms, for example, we ought to have a picture of the nature of those specialisms, a shared language for understanding them, and some direction as to what concrete work can structure curriculum development in those specialisms.

To reiterate, these ideas should be seen as contributions to an ongoing debate rather than ready-made policy. In keeping with this, each chapter is ended with a set of questions for discussion. These may be used for individual reflection, group discussion within a school, or as a prompt for further exploration. The references for each chapter represent a wealth of further reading, and it is hoped that both this and the discourse that is developed as part of curriculum work as recommended in these pages, will be powerful tools in the ongoing journey to which this book seeks to contribute.

1.5.2 Analysis-reduction creep

In curriculum work there is an ever-present danger that we will do well to be aware of and guard against: that of analysis morphing into reductionism. The analysis of complex and challenging entities involved in curriculum – the identification of parts and the discussion of their relations – is very useful. Such analysis can help us to see natures and structures, and to make the implicit explicit. This allows us to have meaningful discussions as professionals, and to plan so that children have the best chance of effectively learning ambitious knowledge. But there is a constant danger of analysis segueing into *reduction*, if we mistake the tools of analysis for sufficient descriptors of reality. As G. E. P. Box said, "all models are wrong but some are useful".[4] Curriculum is irreducible: it functions as a whole, not just a series of pieces, and so we must remember, having gained insight from analysis, to return to the idea of the whole. Thinking about components is useful for understanding but often less so for policy, and there are no short-cuts to intellectual engagement with the subject discourse. To sum up: there are lists in this book, but they are not tick-lists, and we must resist the creep of analysis to reduction at all times.

1.5.3 Deep over surface

There is an ever-present temptation in leadership to pursue surface-level artefacts such as lists, templates, and pro-formas as ends-in-themselves, but this is a mistake where curriculum is concerned. For meaningful curriculum work to take place, there must be thinking: deep, specialist thinking far beyond the superficial. Such thinking must be structured and fed, by reading and discussing with other specialists; *to wit*, by engagement with the discourse. It is the job of senior leaders to bring subject leaders into – to encourage and support – this engagement, and to resist the pull of surface-level work that bypasses the intellectual rigour that is essential for deep and sustained curriculum development. As Christine Counsell has said, "Curriculum development is intricately bound up with teacher development."[5]

1.5.4 Specialist development versus centralised imposition

Some fundamental principles of curriculum theory can shed light on the natures and structures of the specialist subjects. This is not to say that curriculum work at a subject level must *articulate* this theory. Within specialisms, it is certainly possible to have a rich and detailed understanding of one's subject and its structuring in curriculum without reference to particular theoretical terms. Where curriculum theory is developed within a subject discourse it can bring clarity and depth to discussions, but this needs to be carefully built over time in the subject-specific context.

Curriculum theory is, I argue, a necessity of whole-school curriculum *leadership*, since it allows leaders to see clearly the differences in the subjects, and to judge the level of thinking and development priorities within the subjects' curriculum work. There is a fine line between developing specialist work in curriculum theory and imposing jargon on specialists, distracting them from the real business of subject curriculum thinking. In many cases, the specialist discourse is most useful as a guide, so that instead of, for example, senior leaders asking subject leaders to submit a summary of disciplinary knowledge in their subject, a quality article from the discourse on disciplinary knowledge within that subject is read, discussed, and implications for curriculum work agreed and carried out.

It is hoped that those interested in knowledge, curriculum, or school leadership will find much of interest and use in these pages. Senior leaders and governors in particular will be able to apply the ideas discussed here in leading curriculum development in their schools. By engaging with curriculum theory they will be better able to involve subject leaders in high-level curriculum discussion, thinking, planning and execution, and in building and sustaining a culture of continuous engagement with that most wonderful thing: the knowledge in our subjects and the sharing of it with children. Curriculum development can never be complete. The curriculum itself and the orientation of subject leaders towards curricular thinking can certainly be rapidly improved, but following that, the ongoing reading, thinking, and curriculum work by subject leaders and their subject teachers is crucial to the quality of curriculum and teaching in a school. Counsell again puts it best:

> Don't think of the perfect **curriculum** as the goal – think, rather, of a permanent steady state of middle leaders deeply engaged with curricular questions, in a state of continuing **renewal** & ownership of **curriculum**, using that very **renewal** process as ongoing teacher development.[6]

The work of writing this book has often been largely clerical, since so many people have contributed their knowledge and insight, often enduring persistent questioning and correcting my many misconceptions. Without them this book could not have been written, and I am eternally grateful for the help of so many wonderful people. The list of acknowledgements at the end of this book is a wealth of sparkling minds and leading curriculum thinkers, and a treasure trove for anyone seeking individuals to develop their own engagement in the curriculum discourse. Any errors or misrepresentations are of course entirely of my own making, and I very much hope that any that transpire can serve as a starting point for discussion, clarification, and the development of the discourse at the heart of our profession. Education, after all, is a path, and while I have had to educate myself on many, many things in writing this book, there is undoubtedly a great deal more to be done. To all those who have helped me on this stage of my journey, thank you.

Notes

1 Oakeshott (1959), p. 11
2 Ashbee (2020), pp. 34–35
3 Oakeshott (1962), p. 187
4 Box (1976)
5 Counsell (2019a)
6 Counsell (2019b)

References

Ashbee, R. in Sealy, C. (Ed.) *The researchED Guide to the Curriculum*, Ipswich: John Catt, 2020

Box, G. E. P. "Science and Statistics" (PDF), *Journal of the American Statistical Association*, 71 (356), 791–799, 1976

Counsell, C. (2019a), available at https://twitter.com/Counsell_C/status/1099830555166887936; accessed 26.8.2019

Counsell, C. (2019b), available at https://twitter.com/Counsell_C/status/1161557634081796096; accessed 1.08.2019

Oakeshott, M. *The Voice of Poetry in the Conversation of Mankind: An Essay*, London: Bowes and Bowes, 1959

Oakeshott, M. *Rationalism in Politics and Other Essays*, London: Liberty Fund, Inc., 1962

2 CURRICULUM IN CONTEXT

An introduction to curriculum in context

Before we turn to the details of curriculum theory in Chapter 3 – and then some specifics of the subject disciplines in Chapter 4 – some scene-setting is in order. This chapter considers three areas:

- the "Why?" of curriculum, and our moral purpose in pursuing it;

- the very basic "What?" in terms of curriculum and students through the lenses of philosophy and cognitive science;

- and finally, if not quite the "Who?", the question of how to make excellence in curriculum work a reality in the complex, dynamic, cultural, and acutely *human* context of the school.

These three areas form an essential foundation for leadership on the more esoteric material later in these pages.

2.1 The moral imperative

2.1.1 Powerful knowledge

The social realist approach to education "suggests that some knowledge has more power than other knowledge and that access to 'powerful knowledge' should be an entitlement for all children."[1] In *Knowledge and the Future School*, Professor Michael Young develops the social realist approach, characterising two approaches to curriculum, and presenting an alternative model of Powerful Knowledge. Young describes three curricular approaches, or 'futures'. In "Future 1", the curriculum of the traditional grammar and private schools, knowledge for curriculum is seen as fixed and elite, only for the privileged few. In the second model, "Future 2", knowledge is seen as constructed and democratic, with the outcome that no knowledge is better than any other. This model has been charged with lowering standards, particularly for the most disadvantaged, and shutting children out of a valuable education on the basis of nothing more than their socioeconomic status.[2]

Viewed in isolation, these models present a dichotomy, but the dichotomy is false: we need not accept either model. Knowledge is not fixed but that does not mean "anything goes". Ambitious knowledge is intrinsically challenging, but that does not mean it should be reserved for a select group of children. Indeed, now that we know so much more about how to make learning successful,[3] we have no excuse for not bringing all students into a high-reaching and rigorous curriculum. It is possible, and it is morally right.

Young's alternative to Futures 1 and 2 is "Future 3" which takes as its basis the concept of Powerful Knowledge. Powerful Knowledge, in Young's conception, has several key features:

- ▪ "It is distinct from the 'common sense' knowledge we acquire through our everyday experience" – and as such needs to be *taught*.

- ▪ "It is systematic – its concepts are systematically related to each other in groups that we refer to as subjects or disciplines."

- ▪ "It is specialised. In other words [it] is knowledge that has been developed by clearly distinguishable groups, usually occupations, with a clearly defined focus or field of enquiry."[4]

The knowledge in the school curriculum, Young argues, can be shown, or at least argued to be, "best knowledge" through agreement within the subject community. In this way, social realism[5] is invoked to counter the anarchy of relativism, and we can articulate the differentiation we all sense between certain areas of knowledge.[6] For Young, the role of the subject community is paramount[7]– not only in identifying knowledge for curriculum, but also as a curricular object in itself – students should learn about the constructed and mutable nature of knowledge, and not have knowledge presented to them as a finished article, as it is in Future 1.[8] This gives us our distinction between substantive and disciplinary knowledge, which we shall explore in Section 3.3.

The Powerful Knowledge approach is, according to Young,

> not a tool that can tell you what knowledge to include in your classes or how to structure them – that is your responsibility as members of the teaching profession. It is not a curriculum principle in precise terms or the basis of short-term goals or outcomes that can be unambiguously measured.[9]

It is not a formula, but it is a way of looking at curriculum, and a moral starting point for the discussions that must take place, as Young says, within the teaching profession.

In following a social realist approach to curriculum, we are pursuing the empowerment of our students to see beyond the everyday, to transcend the prosaic and make meaning from the world through engagement in the subject disciplines. This, as Young urges, should be the entitlement of all.

Curriculum under this approach, then, has the following aims:

- To provide ambitious and well-chosen knowledge to students so that they may be inducted into the subject disciplines and appreciate the meaning-making that human intellect has developed through those disciplines.

- To provide the curricular basis for a rigorous and far-reaching education that brings all the opportunities that a great education brings: in access to further study, careers, and participation in a democratic society.

- To open up the disciplinary codes for students so that they may learn not only the great claims and contributions of the disciplines, but also their modes of operation, their rules and conventions, so that they may see knowledge and meaning as the products of ongoing discourses: discourses that they are empowered to join, participate in, and challenge as educated people.

2.1.2 Four moral arguments for ambitious curriculum

There are many moral reasons to pursue ambitious curriculum under the Powerful Knowledge approach. Broadly, these fall under four categories:

2.1.2.1 Cognitive

"Knowledge is what we think with and about"[10] and children with more knowledge are better prepared to learn yet more, with knowledge acting as "mental Velcro".[11]

It is now well established within cognitive science that we draw on knowledge whenever we read, think, or solve problems, and that the more and better knowledge we have, the better equipped we are for cognitive work. If we can give students an education rich with well-chosen knowledge, we can help them to become better thinkers, problem solvers, and future learners, with all the benefits these attributes bring.[12]

A common misconception here is that "knowledge" refers merely to isolated facts, when nothing could be further from the truth. The referent of "knowledge" here is everything stored in the long-term memory: including facts, or declarative statements about the world, but also the links between those facts, the relationships and organisation of the propositions, and the meaning that emerges from these. A great deal of knowledge is not in a declarative form at all, but in a tacit or procedural form: we have knowledge of processes and physical skills that we would struggle to articulate, but that nonetheless are significant items in our knowledge-store. The acquisition of all of these forms of knowledge contributes to the knower's ability to intelligently approach future cognitive work in specific and related domains, and also provides a strong foundation on which to build new knowledge, since there are many links that can be made to existing knowledge. In summary: if we teach children Powerful Knowledge, we can make them cleverer.[13]

2.1.2.2 Socioeconomic

Students who have studied a strong curriculum will be better equipped to gain excellent qualifications, pursue careers that demand such qualifications, and access the socioeconomic rewards of these careers. It would be an impoverished society that pursued only these goals in education, but these goals should not be overlooked, and indeed the luxury of overlooking them is, to a large extent, the privilege of the relatively wealthy. The zero-sum game notwithstanding, an education rich in knowledge is a factor in economic success,[14] and we should remember this.

2.1.2.3 Democratic

"Cultural literacy" – an understanding of current affairs and a critical approach to media – is entirely contingent upon knowledge.[15] Students who have studied a powerful curriculum will be better equipped to read and understand news and commentary, to question and challenge ideas, and to participate in a healthy democracy. Indeed, democracy depends on the populace being well-educated in order to keep a check on threats such as fake news, propaganda, and extremism. The ability of people to question the very substance of curriculum, as we have seen with recent work on decolonising the curriculum, for example, depends, rather paradoxically, on knowledge gained one way or another through education, and powerful school curriculum should equip students to bring reasoned challenges of this nature to the table.[16] The role of schools and curriculum then, in free society, must not be underestimated.

2.1.2.4 Intellectual

Since civilisation first began, people have sought to make meaning in the world.[17] People have brought forth beauty, described truth, and created ingenious responses to the problems of living in the material world. This knowledge has passed down through the generations, growing, changing, bringing awe, delight, and progress to those it touches. It is a wonderful thing, and it should be the societal entitlement of every child, from every household and every background, to learn about this knowledge, and to learn how to participate in the disciplines that bear such wonderful fruit. Future generations deserve to have this knowledge treasured and passed on so that the fires are burning brightly for them when it is their turn. And great thinkers of the past – many of whom suffered vilification, ridicule, even death for their pursuit of knowledge and beauty – these intellectual ancestors of ours deserve to have their work kept alight. It is in schools and curriculum that the torches of knowledge are housed, and their light should shine on all children.

2.1.3 "Whose knowledge?"

The question of how "best knowledge" is identified and narrowed down to fit the constraints of the school curriculum is an important one. While Young's conception of the subject community as arbiter is strong, it is not complete. What if the subject community has disagreements within its ranks? What are we to make of changes in the subject community? Whig history, for example, dominated that discipline for some time before understanding developed. Indeed, almost by definition, change to the establishment must come from outside the establishment. A goal of complete consensus as to the detail of what knowledge should be included in curriculum, particularly given the very finite nature of time in schools, is probably necessarily unattainable, but this should not be cause for despair.

Firstly, there are probably a great many formulations that are good, and it is certainly possible to reach agreement that some things are better than others; where thought has been given to the justification of content within curriculum, the result will almost certainly be better than where no such discussion has been had. Returning to our moral purposes of education, we should choose best bets over stabs in the dark, even when absolute certainty or agreement is an impossibility. Second, the discussion is ongoing and iterative. Curriculum must not be written in tablets of stone: while some is statutory and much is codified in examination specifications, textbooks, and so on, none of these things are immutable. They exist as they do today as the direct result of discussion between academics, teachers, and policymakers, and that discussion is a crucial part of a democratic society.[18] As Young himself points out, knowledge is not fixed – it is constructed and built by people, and the same is true of curriculum. The continued discourse and the shaping of curriculum over time, and the presence of teachers in this conversation, are vital. There is not an implicit compulsion to accept the status quo; in fact, the opposite is true.

If we consider the knowledge in our disciplines to be something to be treasured, we would do well to listen to Oakeshott: "Nothing survives in this world which is not cared for by human beings."[19] This caring is as we do for a garden, not a fragile ornament – it must be fed, and this is (Oakeshott again) "impossible without a diversity of voices".[20]

2.2 Building knowledge: curriculum and the knower

2.2.1 Knowledge and curriculum

The nature of knowledge and knowers has interested thinkers throughout the ages. The term epistemology, or theory of knowledge, comes to us from the ancient Greeks, and ever since its inception, philosophers have argued over the nature of knowledge and knowing. The classical definition of knowledge as "justified true belief" is beset with problems, since both truth and justification are almost always impossible to prove. Questions of truth are important for curriculum work, both in our considerations of what should be included[21] and in our planning for teaching students about the nature of truth-claims within the subjects, since this is a key part of the Powerful Knowledge approach. Fortunately, the difficulties with the concept of knowledge need not be an impediment to curriculum work, and the term is more usually used to mean "material to be learned" or "material that has been learned". At the end of their time with us in school, we want our students to leave with certain things: understandings, abilities, ways of seeing the world... all of these can – should – be grouped under the term "knowledge".

In order to reach this point – to acquire all this knowledge – students follow a curriculum, or course.[22] The knowledge we want them to leave with must be constructed over time, with strands, components, and progressions, with exercises to build ability, and developing knowledge that can be successfully built on throughout the journey. Curriculum, then, is knowledge structured over time.[23]

This structuring, however, is often not straightforward, since *the means of nurture often do not resemble the final product.*[24] Often a significant part of "structuring knowledge over time" is the identification of components of knowledge and exercises to develop abilities that do not look like the knowledge we wish students to leave with – so in art for example we may find multiple measurement exercises, and in English, work on single sentences: we are not just cutting up the final knowledge and pasting it onto a timeline. We are building schemata, webs of organised knowledge in long-term memory, and doing so is complex.

2.2.2 Insights from theorists

While philosophers and sociologists may not have solved the question of knowledge, there are nevertheless many important insights about knowledge and knowers to be taken from these fields. Several theorists are of particular interest here:

Michael Oakeshott: The idea of learning as an intensely human activity is articulated beautifully by Oakeshott. From him we get the phrase "the great conversations of mankind"; learning, for Oakeshott, is "the comprehensive engagement in which we come to know ourselves and the world around us."[25] Through education and the subject disciplines, according to Oakeshott, meaning is made both for the individual and for humanity over time. Crucial to this understanding is the distinctness of the subject disciplines, illuminated through Oakeshott's *modes of experience.*

Michael Polanyi: Polanyi emphasises the personal nature of knowledge, and the role of the knower and their commitment or involvement. He characterises this commitment as an indwelling or living-in: when we use a theory, language, or idea, we reach out into the world with it in the same way that

> the skilful use of a tool actually identifies it to an important extent with our own body. The rower pulling an oar feels its blade tearing the water; when using a paper-knife we feel its edge cutting the pages.[26]

This idea illuminates the value of the subject disciplines, as extensions of ourselves, as implements of indwelling. It is also a useful reminder when we seek to characterise the differences in the subjects in order to treat them justly: what is indwelling *like* in this subject? How does it differ from the indwelling in other subjects?

Martin Heidegger: Heidegger's key idea is *dasein* or being-in-the-world, and that the self is made in part of our experience of, and relations with, things in the world: with practical or useful things, with theoretical things, and with other people.[27] This conception of the self leads us to the essential preciousness of knowledge, and its inseparableness from our notions of our own existence.

Edmund Husserl: From Husserl we take the concept of the Lebenswelt or lifeworld, a world of shared understanding inhabited by people in their mutual knowledge of things. For Husserl, this lifeworld is the foundation from which all other enquiry about knowledge must proceed.[28] For our thinking about curriculum, we can draw from this insight into the meaning of operating within a specialism, of being a member of a discipline, and of participating in an ongoing discourse.

Gilbert Ryle: In Ryle's work we find a characterisation of declarative and procedural knowledge as knowing-that and knowing-how respectively. Ryle claims that knowing-how is logically prior to knowing-that, and that the former cannot be expressed in terms of the latter.[29] This gives us a powerful tool for thinking about curriculum and powerful knowledge: it is only by undergoing processes and engaging in things over time that we can come to know about things.

Michel Foucault: We come next to Foucault, who gives us the idea of *gaze*, of particular ways of looking, unique to specialisms, professions or positions, and conferring a power on the looker to notice and experience certain things.[30] It is not only in the detail, nature, and structure and operations of the knowledge in the subjects that their character resides, but in this less specifiable and more rarefied gaze that a knower turns on the world when authentically participating in a subject.

Basil Bernstein: Focusing now more on the knowledge itself, Bernstein's work has been seminal in the description of the organisation, structure, and relations in knowledge, through his conceptions of, among other things, hierarchical and horizontal knowledge.[31] Section 3.4 builds on this work, towards a coherent theory of relations of knowledge.

Karl Maton: The work of Karl Maton and the Legitimation Code Theory programme has developed many important analyses of knowledge and disciplines, allowing sophisticated comparisons between areas with regard to the nature of their knowledge, the methods of knowledge approval, the interconnectedness of the knowledge, and many other key characteristics.[32] These analyses inform much of Chapter 3.

Etienne Wenger: Wenger posits, in his *Communities of Practice*, that

> human engagement in the world is first and foremost a process of negotiating meaning [...] The concept of negotiation often denotes reaching an agreement between people, as in "negotiating a price," but it is not limited to that usage. It is also used to suggest an accomplishment that requires sustained attention and readjustment, as in "negotiating a sharp curve." [...] I intend the term *negotiation* to convey a flavor of continuous interaction, of gradual achievement, and of give-and-take. By living in the world we do not just make meanings up independently of the world, but neither does the world simply impose meanings on us. The negotiation of meaning is a productive process, but negotiating meaning is not constructing it from scratch. Meaning is not pre-existing, but neither is it simply made up. Negotiated meaning is at once both historical and dynamic, contextual and unique.

This sense of meaning as an ongoing and dynamic experience, formed by people in their interactions both at the frontiers of knowledge as researchers or other producers, and as reproducers of knowledge as students and apprentices, is key to our exploration of curriculum in this book.[33]

2.2.3 Insights from cognitive science

Since curriculum is intended to be learned and used, and since both learning and using knowledge are cognitive activities, it follows that we can draw upon the field of cognitive science in order to inform our work.

2.2.3.1 Types of memory

Cognitive science often groups memory into categories. Declarative memory comprises both episodic and semantic memory, or (crudely) experiences and facts respectively, while procedural (or non-declarative) memory is the often implicit memory of processes or techniques.[34] There are obvious and important parallels here with Ryle's knowing-that and knowing-how, and such distinctions are useful in helping developing thinking about the components (see Section 3.3) and progression (Section 3.5) of curriculum, and for identifying the effective practice or work for developing students' abilities and acquisition of knowledge (Section 5.2).

2.2.3.2 Cognitive architecture and models

Baddeley and Hitch's[35] model of learning characterises our cognitive architecture as comprising a limited working memory and an almost limitless long-term memory, from which knowledge must be retrieved in order to be used by the working memory.[36] In the long-term memory, knowledge is conceived of as being stored in schemata: webs of connected ideas, whose organisation carries meaning.[37] We also build prototypes of ideas from exposure to examples, and can make use of chunking information by linking pieces together and thereby allowing our working memory to treat them as one item.[38]

The details of these models have been thoroughly explicated elsewhere;[39] let us now consider what some of the implications for curriculum work might be.

2.2.3.3 Implications for curriculum work

Cognitively, the aim of curriculum work is to plan actions that will allow students to develop their schemata for the subject in question. In doing this work we must explore our own schemata, and consider what insights we might gain for supporting our students in this building and strengthening of schemata, *to wit*, their learning.

In planning and mapping curriculum, we must consider, among other things, how to manage the "cognitive load" of students, avoiding an "overload" of the working memory, and planning for the acquisition to fluency of various components before asking students to combine them in challenging syntheses. Thus, for example, we might teach various types of sentence and argumentation, as well as a set of declarative facts, before we begin teaching the construction of an essay argument in religious studies, for example. These ideas are explored in Sections 3.5 and 3.6.

In the detail of our planning of content, we might bear these ideas in mind when codifying our explanations, examples, and non-examples,[40] and the type of work or practice we will set for students in order for them to build their own schemata, prototypes, and chunkings (meaningful groupings of information). In Chapter 5 we begin to explore these aspects of the codification of the detail of curriculum content. There will also be implications for our planning of things like retrieval practice, so that students' ability to retrieve knowledge from their store in long-term memory is strengthened, and assessment for learning, so that we can be sure of the correct pre-requisite knowledge in security, in order to allow students to build effective schemata.

In all of this, it is vital that the subject specialisms lead the application of theory, and not the other way round. It is not enough to have "retrieval practice" or "components" in all subjects, that is to say, the nature of these things must be appropriate to the subject in question and may look very different across specialisms. There are no short-cuts: subject-specific curriculum thinking must always take precedence.

The nature of knowledge and knowers is a fascinating and rich area for exploration; informing our thinking through philosophy and cognitive science is an intellectually responsible approach to such a significant issue in education; and we must then close the loop through the pursuit of recontextualisation in the subject specialisms: "What should this look like for *this* subject?"

2.3 A culture of curriculum

Excellence in curriculum work is not an easy, quick, or simple thing to achieve. It is demanding. It relies on informed and thoughtful people, working hard, in an environment where thinking can thrive. In many schools, a shift to work of this nature requires a step-change in the approaches and behaviours of staff and the systems which structure the school.

School culture is a mysterious thing: palpable in its presence, hard to define, vitally important. To enter into ambitious curriculum work without an explicit consideration of – and strategy for – developing the right school culture for this work to flourish, would be a fool's errand, destined to fail. Culture can be analysed, planned for, and intentionally built. This is the job of school leaders.

2.3.1 The cultural backdrop of the school

Let us start with a picture of a successful culture of curriculum. In schools where this obtains, lessons are free from disruption. Teachers plan for their subject and the learning of the children, and not for anything else. They work hard, with commitment and joy. Teachers are encouraged to be simultaneously confident in their place in the school and aware of teaching as a never-ending developmental activity, where reflection, discussion, and engagement with wider subject discourse are constant sources of change to one's practice. This wider discourse can be understood as the body of work, thought, and discussion around the subject, in books, journals, the subject associations, conference presentations, social media, and so on. It is at the heart of all curriculum work.

Departments in schools with a culture of curriculum meet often to discuss, not administration or generic policies, but their own subject, its discourse, their own planning, and reflections on their teaching, and the quality of these conversations rivals those in the most elite institutions. Staff read, and read, and read. They actively engage in the subject discourse, through conferences, subject networks, and social media. Such schools are exciting and rewarding places to work and attract highly intelligent, committed staff.

This culture does not arise spontaneously; nor is it some magic for which only some schools have the secret. It is an emergent property of a school with intelligent and genuine curriculum-focused leadership and it is attainable everywhere. It is built from structures, policies, attention to detail, and authenticity.

A culture of curriculum is one of unashamed intellectualism. This is not to say that the pace and pragmatism of school leadership should be neglected (this is not the intellectualism of the carefree Parisian coffee shop or the languorous university common room.) It is to say that staff are encouraged and supported to engage in intellectual activity, in their reading and involvement with the subject community, in their planning and their teaching. This encouragement and support are manifest in the fundamental structures in the school and are modelled with authenticity from the top: leaders immerse themselves in reading widely and engage in both subject and leadership discourse.

In such schools, the only limitation on teachers' engagement with their subject, and their planning and teaching of it, is the finitude of time. Any and all activity that does not contribute to either curriculum, learning, or school culture has been disposed of. Performative practice is nowhere, and time is spent on doing important things, not "evidencing" that they have done them. Leaders seek information, they work out a way of finding out what they want to know that does not take staff away from their duties as curriculum thinkers and teachers. Leaders lead for excellent behaviour, with all the structures and enactment that make that a reality in every classroom. Systems that distort subjects, such as generic teaching and learning, assessment, or performance management policies, have been done away with. [41]

In these schools, no teacher ever has to choose between teaching their subject well and scoring highly on some checklist on a clipboard: there is no conflict between policy and what works best for each subject. Expectations and accountability are high, sky-high in fact, since ambitious curriculum demands such, but the curriculum in the specialisms itself dictates the forms and details of those exigencies and methodologies: subjects remain true to themselves.

The importance of discourse has already been mentioned above. It should be a defining feature of all centres of intellectual work, in universities, industry, and schools, that people challenge each other, and are themselves open to challenge, without fear or hesitation. In schools this is a rare cultural characteristic, and it is worth considering why this might be.

"Means-end analysis" is something of an assumed truth in the school improvement lexicon, but it can be responsible for a culture averse to the continued discourse needed for excellence in curriculum work. In this model, a final goal or end-point is described, and the component steps identified, planned, and executed in order to achieve the desired outcome. While this is *prima facie* a sensible approach, it is problematic because it rests on, and encourages, the tacit assumption that an end point exists, and that, until that point is reached, things are not as they should be. The logical conclusions from this are that 1) those who are good at their jobs are a finished article and don't need to develop further, and 2) any developments are in themselves an assertion of incompleteness or poor quality. The reflection of this approach in high-stakes performance management systems only serves to reinforce the paradigm. This approach is utterly at odds with the essence of curriculum work.

Curriculum work is never finished, it is never completed: it is – or should be – a never-ending and essential activity at the core of teaching, and must be understood as something to participate in as practice, rather than something to be achieved and then left. The highly cerebral and dynamic nature of curriculum work means that challenge and debate are crucial, and the mindset to welcome these must acknowledge, account for, and mitigate against ego and insecurity. None of this is to say that goals, planning, and evaluation do not play an important role in school leadership: they do. But the paradigm of continuous development as a characteristic of the very best practitioners must be explicitly planned for, communicated, and nurtured. The best cultures marry pride in the level of intellectual work with humility at the size of the domain and the understanding that we can never know everything there is to know, and that we will never finish this most wonderful of tasks.

Culture is hard to get right. It must be manifest in organisational details in order to take hold in the psyches of people and influence autonomous and authentic behaviour. Culture becomes reality when it permeates an organisation, when it is lived and reflected throughout, and to achieve this permeation, the consonance or dissonance of every part of school life with the intended cultural principles must be considered and aligned. Strong culture in a school often looks like either good luck or sorcery; in reality it is there for any who choose to pursue it. However, it requires boldness, thoroughness, and attention to detail, but none of these should be strangers to school leadership, and as a foundation for curriculum work, culture is utterly indispensable.

2.3.2 Engagement with the subject discourse

Let us turn now to the nature of what we have termed "engagement with the subject discourse". As argued above, the subject discourse is the body of discussion and thought held in all the books, blogs, journals, conference presentations, and less formal discussions between people face-to-face and on social media. Engagement in this discourse refers to the reading of this work, the discussion thereof, and the development of work and practice in light of this reading and thought.

Such engagement is important for several reasons. Firstly, there are many and significant benefits both to the curriculum and to teaching within the school. To be able to build on the thinking of others in the field often brings immediate and far-reaching developments for departments. Beyond that, teachers themselves undergo fundamental and sustained intellectual development through this engagement, with rewards to be reaped in an ongoing sense as they bring new insight to their future work as teachers in the school. Such engagement is a powerful motivator, addictive even, and where it is encouraged, the development and retention of high-quality staff is powerfully served. The alignment of staff within department teams, and the sharing of a common language and professional ideology, so important for successful organisations, are fed by the sharing of readings and discussions. Within the broader school culture, departments have their own cultures, and these are built partly on this shared subject discourse within them.

Beyond the school, there are yet more reasons to engage with subject discourse. As staff develop and flourish in their curriculum thinking, they will themselves be able to make important contributions to the discourse, and from this work in turn other teachers, their curricula, and ultimately, their students can grow. As we saw in Section 2.1, the democratic imperative for an active subject discourse is real. As such this engagement can be seen as, ultimately, a professional responsibility of teachers, viewing the work of schools through a wider, societal lens.

This engagement with the discourse should not be left to arise spontaneously, but should be led across a whole staff. There needs to be leadership of the selection of the content itself that is engaged with, *to wit*, the articles, books, blogs and so on that are read and discussed within a department. This leadership may at times need to be directive; at others it might seek to curate, steer, or merely need to be kept informed of the content. The type of leadership required will depend on the knowledge and stage of department leadership and staff, but also the field itself. In some subjects the discourse is so rich and well-developed it can be hard to know where to start, in others there is very little in terms of rich curriculum thinking, while in others still there is a wide diversity of approaches that will require navigation in alignment with the school. The involvement of subject specialists will be critical here and finding a specialist who can advise on the best areas to pursue, someone with excellent curriculum thinking and experience, is invaluable to informing this leadership.

A particular challenge arises where the wider subject discourse is not yet very developed in terms of curriculum thinking. There may be excellent discourse to be found, but it must be sought out. Individual specialists from schools with similar curriculum ambitions are an invaluable resource here,[42] and books from the field of production, or from higher and further education, or even sometimes from the teach-yourself genre, can be significant sources of discourse content. Indeed, Young places a great deal of responsibility in the subject community – so we must build, develop, and shape the subject communities if we are committed to powerful knowledge curriculum for our students.

Of course, the sourcing of key pieces from the subject discourse is only part of the story. What is done with these elements is equally crucial, and something that will need to be structured or led to a greater or lesser extent, depending on the context of each subject department. Giving staff time to read, think about specific questions or discussion points, and then discuss their responses and the implications for curriculum is a powerful model. The substance of the questions and implications can be guided and/or discussed with leadership depending on the priorities of the department. As a response to readings and ensuing discussions, for example, departments may make decisions about sequencing, ways of explanation, work to develop students' understanding, and so on. These changes to practice can form fruitful bases for discussions between senior leaders and both subject leaders and classroom teachers, and such conversations serve both to strengthen clarity of thought in specialists and to build understanding in non-specialist leadership.

So far, we have discussed reactive engagement with discourse, where the engager absorbs and recontextualises ideas from material already in existence – but of course discourse is a dialectic, and as staff read, think, and reflect, they will develop their own thinking which can in turn feed valuable contributions to the conversation. The encouragement of staff to put forth their work, to share thinking, to blog, write for subject journals, to share resources for discussion and to speak at conferences, is a potent tool for development and engagement of staff. More broadly, this work is a part of the vital, organic, in-flux nature of discourse and can also be structured and led. School leaders should seek opportunities to encourage teachers to blog, or to invite them to write for a school blog or journal if they would prefer not to host their own. Additionally, leaders might consider working with staff to submit and plan conference presentations, to support those first steps and structure this often overlooked area of teachers' professional development.

2.3.3 An informed leadership

As outlined in Chapter 1, there is a paradox at the heart of curriculum leadership: the need for central leaders to guide and monitor the work of departments, and the prioritising of subject specialisms over genericism. Since no leader can be a specialist in all subjects, we arrive at an apparent impasse. The curation, guidance, and discussion of the specialist engagement with subject discourse is of course a vital key to overcoming this contradiction, but can only take us so far.

In order to lead this engagement, those leading must themselves have a degree of understanding of the specialisms and their discourses. There are no shortcuts to this understanding; the subject sections in this book offer a brief introduction, and further understanding can only be built by further reading of blogs, books, and journals; through attending specialist sessions at education conferences; and through engaging in discussion, in particular in asking questions, of specialists both within and beyond the school. And as this specialist understanding is built, it is vital that a concomitant awareness of the limits of this understanding is also established. The trap of "a little knowledge being a dangerous thing" must be avoided. Non-specialists are not consigned to an eternity of ignorance – they can and indeed must seek greater understanding – but this development must not be misunderstood to be an acquisition of specialism. Wise curriculum leadership recognises that subject specialist expertise takes years of dedicated study.

2.3.4 Curriculum must be lived

A fascinating thing about great curriculum is its resistance to being "bought in". Although there are departments in schools and trusts working on truly excellent curriculum, however much other departments would like to simply pick up this work and use it, there is always significant loss unless that second department has engaged in curriculum thinking of sufficient depth and breadth. Even within a single department, when curriculum work is produced by one member of staff and just shared almost at the point of use, without time given to curriculum discussion, the work inevitably falls short of its original value in the hands of its creator/s.

The reasons for this difficulty in transfer are cognitive, social, and cultural. Curriculum is about knowledge structured over time, about doing things in classrooms to build meaning in students. The choices made by a curriculum writer reflect the writer's own schema: the items and links that stand out, the logical relations that take priority, the exemplars that fit perfectly *for that writer*. While all expert schemas about a field will have many features in common, they must necessarily have some features apart because of the personal nature of knowledge, because of the detail – usually tacit – of the knower's own experience.

This is not to say that all, or even most, departments should create their own curricula from scratch. There are several ways to save reinvention of wheels. In trusts where it is possible to employ a subject lead, a central curriculum can be developed alongside close work with departments in the subject. In other schools and trusts, it is possible to buy in the materials for great curricula from external sources and translate them into great curricula but *only if the department spends significant time and thought with the curriculum materials*. Ideally, this work would be undertaken with ongoing guidance from the original developers, thinking through the logic and unfolding of the curriculum as manifested in those materials, and – crucially – making educated adjustments where the department feels it will allow better meaning to be made in their context.

Context here has nothing to do with the unique socioeconomic, geographical, or historical details of the placement of a school, and everything to do with the fact that knowledge is personal. The details that make expert schemas non-identical means that a curriculum will be forced and incomplete if there are clashes between how people feel a curriculum should unfold and a document which tells them to follow a different path. For many departments, the best course of action will be to write their own curriculum, creating a narrative that is grown organically from the department itself, but drawing on resources from external sources.

The unifying feature of all these possibilities is the need for the investment of time and scholarly conversation, within departments, about the substance of what is to be taught and the logic of the piecing, explanations, and sequencing. Although this work is critical it is unlikely to "just happen". This is where senior leadership must assist in the development of culture and thought, and the time required for these things, within departments. The development of a culture of curriculum requires three things: fertile conditions for such a culture, informed senior leadership, and engagement with the subject discourse. All of this can – and must – be intentionally led.

2.4 Conclusion to the chapter

We have seen now that there is an urgent moral imperative to the effective leadership of ambitious and powerful curriculum for all students, regardless of their background, and that in cognitive research we can find both support for this view ("knowledge is what we think with") and guidance for how to ensure that ambitious knowledge is effectively learned and remembered. The role of school leaders in developing curriculum work in schools must be understood as the fundamental business of school leadership, and inseparable from the intentional development of culture, since excellence in curriculum work is both intellectually demanding and a significant departure from the comfortable modes of working for many staff. This leadership role can only be executed well when informed by an understanding of a theory of knowledge and of the specialist subjects themselves: the focus of the following two chapters.

2.5 Questions for discussion

2.5.1 The moral imperative

■ What do you see as the moral purpose of your school? Is this vision shared? What work might need to be undertaken to develop a shared purpose?

■ How does Future 3 deal with philosophical objections to truth and fixed knowledge?

- Why might good intentions in the past have led to low expectations for students from disadvantaged backgrounds?

- What is the role of cognitive science in the moral imperative for ambitious curriculum?

- Why is it important to consider "Whose knowledge"? What role can teachers play in this discussion?

2.5.2 Building curriculum: curriculum and the knower

- What does planning curriculum to manage cognitive load look like?

- How should curriculum for this subject build retrieval strength?

- How should checks on prerequisite learning be built into this curriculum?

- What are the features of an effective schema for this area of the curriculum? How should students be supported in developing such a schema?

2.5.3 A culture of curriculum

- What policies, practices and habits can promote a culture of intellectualism and curriculum in a school? What things need to be removed or changed?

- How are the subject specialisms protected from genericism and distortion within the school?

- How do the policies and practices within the school promote a culture of discussion, challenge, and reflection, and continuous development as an end in itself?

- What are the key areas for the discourse in this subject?

- Which specialists beyond the school can be asked for guidance?

- What is the nature of the curriculum discourse for this subject? Is it highly developed, diverse, or nascent? How should this be navigated?

- What is the context of this department? Should some suggested readings be put forward? How should these be curated?

- How should discussions of, and developments from, readings be structured and managed within departments?

- How should leadership keep abreast of these discussions and developments without creating additional work for departments?

▪ What readings should leadership undertake in order to begin to develop understandings of specialisms?

▪ Which staff should be encouraged to join active contributions to the discourse? What support should they be given?

Notes

1 Young and Lambert (2014) p. 71
2 Ashbee (2019)
3 See, for example, Willingham (2010)
4 Young and Lambert (2014) pp. 74–75
5 See, for example, Wheelahan (2010)
6 This approach is not without its problems however; see Young (2007) pp. 23–24
7 [7] See "Engagement with the subject discourse" in 2.3 below.
8 Young and Lambert (2014) p. 59
9 Young (2020) p. 27
10 Didau (2017) and Didau (2019) pp. 175–188
11 Hirsch (2018)
12 See e.g. Willingham (2010), Christodoulou (2014) and Hirsch (2000)
13 See, for example, Didau (2019)
14 The Office For National Statistics (2011)
15 See Hirsch (2020)
16 Counsell 2018a
17 See Oakeshott (1989)
18 Ashbee (2020)
19 Oakeshott (1965) p. 42
20 Oakeshott (1959) p. 490
21 See Mountstevens (2020)
22 Indeed the word "curriculum" is Latin for "running, course, career"
23 Counsell 2018b
24 Christodoulou (2016) p. 45
25 Oakeshott (1965) p. 35
26 Polanyi (1962)
27 Heidegger (1927) (1953)
28 Husserl (1936) pp. 108–109
29 Ryle (1945)
30 Foucault (1977) p. 184
31 Bernstein (1999)
32 Maton (2014)
33 Wenger (1998) pp. 53–54
34 See Roediger et al. (2008) and Neath and Surprenant (2015)
35 Baddeley and Hitch (1974)
36 See Willingham (2010) p. 55
37 Reif (2010) Ch. 9
38 Rugg and Gerrard (2014)
39 See, for example, Willingham (2010) and Kirschner, Sweller and Clark (2006)
40 See Percival (2019) and Engelmann (1982)

41 Counsell (2016)
42 Although beware the dangers of mimetic isomorphism: see https://www.tandfonline.
    com/doi/abs/10.1080/13632434.2017.1293633?src=recsys&journalCode=cslm20&

References

Ashbee, R. "Powerful Knowledge: What It Is, Why It's Important, And How To Make It Happen In Your School", *The Fruits Are Sweet*, 2019, available at https://www.ruth-ashbee.com/post/powerful-knowledge-what-it-is-why-it-s-important-and-how-to-make-it-happen-in-your-school (accessed 11.12.2019)

Ashbee, R. "Why It's So Important to Understand School Subjects – And How we Might Begin To Do So", in Sealy, C. (Ed.) *The researchED Guide to the Curriculum*. Ipswich: John Catt, 2020

Baddeley, A. and Hitch, G. "Working Memory", in G.H. Bower (Ed.), *The Psychology of Learning and Motivation: Advances in Research and Theory*, Vol. 8, pp. 47–89. New York: Academic Press, 1974

Bernstein, B. "Vertical and Horizontal Discourse: An Essay", in *British Journal of Sociology of Education*, 20, 157–173, 1999

Christodoulou, D. *Seven Myths About Education*. Abingdon: Routledge, 2014

Christodoulou, D. *Making Good Progress?* Oxford Oxford University Press, 2016

Counsell, C. "Genericism's Children", *The Dignity of the Thing*, 2016, available at https://thedignityofthethingblog.wordpress.com/2016/01/11/genericisms-children/ (accessed 2.01.20)

Counsell, C. (2018a) "Senior Curriculum Leadership 1: The Indirect Manifestation of Knowledge: (A) Curriculum as Narrative", *The Dignity of the Thing*, 2018, available at https://thedignityofthethingblog.wordpress.com/2018/04/07/senior-curriculum-leadership-1-the-indirect-manifestation-of-knowledge-a-curriculum-as-narrative/ (accessed 17.2.2020)

Counsell, C. "Taking Curriculum Seriously", in *Impact – Journal of the Chartered College of Teaching*, 4, 2018b, available at: https://impact.chartered.college/article/taking-curriculum-seriously/ (accessed 13.02.2020)

Didau, D. "If Not Knowledge, What?", *David Didau*, 2017, available at https://learningspy.co.uk/featured/if-not-knowledge-what/ (accessed 13.02.2020)

Didau, D. *Making Kids Cleverer*. Carmarthen: Crown House, 2019

Engelmann, S. *Theory of Instruction: Principles and Applications*. New York: Irvington, 1982

Foucault, M. *Discipline and Punish: The Birth of the Prison*. New York: Random House, 1977

Hirsch, E. 2000. https://www.semanticscholar.org/paper/Ifty-eight-Years-Ago-When-I-Was-in-Ninth-Grade%2C-I-a-Hirsch/bfae3f4388acbf0bc46b70767e2b0e70c2049259?p2d)

Hirsch, E. *Why Knowledge Matters*. Cambridge, MA: Harvard University Press, 2018

Hirsch, E. *How to Educate a Citizen*. Ipswich: John Catt, 2020

Heidegger, M. *Being and Time* (Stambaugh, J). Albany: State University of New York Press, 1927/1953

Husserl, E. *The Crisis of the European Sciences*. Illinois: Northwestern University Press, 1936/1970

Kirschner, P., Sweller, J. and Clark, R. "Why Minimal Guidance During Instruction Does Not Work", in *Educational Psychologist* 41(2), 2006

Maton, K. *Knowledge and Knowers*. Abingdon: Routledge, 2014

Mountstevens, J. "Truthfulness and Cultural Literacy", *Occam's Hairdryer*, 2020, available at https://occamshairdryer.wordpress.com/2020/08/15/truthfulness-and-cultural-literacy/ (accessed 20.08.2020)

Neath, I. and Surprenant, A. "Proactive Interference", in *International Encyclopedia of the Social & Behavioral Sciences* (2nd Edition). London: Elsevier, 2015

Oakeshott, M. *The Voice of Poetry in the Conversation of Mankind*. London: Bowes and Bowes, 1959

Oakeshott, M. "Learning and Teaching" in *The Voice of Liberal Learning*. Indiana: Yale, 1965/1989

Oakeshott, M. *The Voice of Liberal Learning*. Indiana: Yale, 1989

The Office for National Statistics, Earnings By Qualification 2011, 2011, available at https://www.nationalarchives.gov.uk/documents/f0048492-office-of-national-statistics-report.pdf, (accessed 15.08.2020)

Percival, A. "Three Ways to Tackle Common Pupil Misconceptions", *The Times Educational Supplement*, 2019, available at https://www.tes.com/news/3-ways-tackle-common-pupil-misconceptions (accessed 5.02.2020)

Polanyi, M. "Tacit Knowing: Its Bearing on Some Problems of Philosophy", in *Review of Modern Physics* 34 (4), October 1962, available at http://faculty.uml.edu/rinnis/45.301%20Ways%20of%20Knowing/Tacit%20Knowing.htm (accessed 05.02.2020)

Reif, F. *Applying Cognitive Science to Education*. Massachusetts: MIT Press, 2010

Roediger, H.L., Zaromb, F.M. and Goode, M.K. "A Typology of Memory Terms", in J.H. Byrne (Ed.) *Learning and Memory: A Comprehensive Reference*. London: Elsevier, 2008

Rugg, G. and Gerrard, S. "Chunking, Schemata and Prototypes", *Hyde and Rugg*, 2014, available at https://hydeandrugg.wordpress.com/2014/07/08/chunking-schemata-and-prototypes/ (accessed 20.08.20)

Ryle, G. "Knowing How and Knowing That", in *Proceedings of the Aristotelian Society*, 46, pp. 1–16. 1945–1946

Walker, M.P. "Sleep-dependent Memory Processing", in L.R. Squire (Ed.) *Encyclopedia of Neuroscience*. London: Elsevier, 2009

Wenger, E. *Communities of Practice*. Cambridge: Cambridge University Press, 1998

Wheelahan, L. *Why Knowledge Matters in Curriculum*. Abingdon: Routledge, 2010

Willingham, D. *Why Don't Students Like School?*. San Francisco: Jossey-Bass, 2010

Young, M. *Bringing Knowledge Back In*. London: Routledge 2007

Young, M. and Lambert, D. *Knowledge and the Future School*. London: Bloomsbury, 2014

Young, M. "From Powerful Knowledge to the Powers of Knowledge", in Sealy, C. (Ed.) *The researchED Guide to the Curriculum*. John Catt: Ipswich, 2020

3 CURRICULUM THEORY

An introduction to curriculum theory

Schools are in the business of knowledge, and so it follows that school leadership should draw on theories of knowledge. Regrettably, such theories have been largely absent from much of the school leadership discourse over the years. This chapter lays out some components that might begin to form a body of curriculum theory, to allow insight, bring clarity to thought, create a common language for discussion, and allow the differences between the subjects to be seen more clearly. In this way, leadership of curriculum can be strengthened and a more productive discourse developed.

Three established academic areas are of use to a theory of curriculum:

- Ontology, or the study of concepts and ideas in a body of meaning, and the relations between them

- Epistemology, or the study of the ways in which knowledge is reached, and the nature of knowing

- Sociology, in particular Legitimation Code Theory and social realism, and the study of the interactions between people, the world, and knowledge, particularly within the subject disciplines.

This chapter draws and builds on these three fields, seeking to contribute something of a starting point for a theory of curriculum, in the hope of better-informed curriculum leadership and developing discourse.

Curriculum theory for specialists

To the specialist, a theory of one's own curriculum is vital. In curriculum work, with each subject we are handling a body of knowledge with its own rules and characteristics, a system with its own grammar, syntax, and semantics. Being able to see the nature of these things facilitates the work of curriculum thinking in the same way that a knowledge of anatomy helps the artist to draw. Being able to give names to things, such as substantive and disciplinary knowledge, core and hinterland, declarative and procedural, helps to identify them, and only when these things have been properly identified can they be really well thought about and planned for. The school curriculum carries so much more meaning, represents so much more majesty and depth, than the words in the specifications or whatever the ostensible starting points might be. It is a vital link: a link between the discipline, the entirety of the work of all those wonderful thinkers over the centuries and millennia, and the next stage of the human race. None of us will live forever, but through the process of education, knowledge can. In seeing the nature of a discipline, it is possible to engage with the enormity of the task and to build curriculum with all the thought and meaning it deserves.

For some subjects, the existing discourse already contains a highly sophisticated theory of curriculum, developed by teachers and other educators through their participation in that discourse, in journal articles, blogs, and other discussions. For other subjects, theories of curriculum have not yet been widely articulated. This need not mean that curriculum thinking in these subjects must be stymied, although it might mean some pioneering work is required. In Chapter 4, some suggestions are made for how curriculum in the specialisms might be interpreted using some of the theory laid out here. It is hoped that these suggestions can feed into developing and continuing discourse and help to build specialist curriculum theory where it is still nascent.

Curriculum theory for generalists

To the generalist, such as the senior leader, a general theory of curriculum is important as well as a degree of understanding of specialisms. Abstract concepts are useful precisely because they can condense down out of the ether into one of many more concrete forms. In comparison lies insight, as the eighteenth-century anatomist Georges Cuvier knew. Features that are normally hidden become clear when we study one thing against another. The essential tension between subject specialism and whole-school generalism, requires a mediation, a translation of sorts (though necessarily incomplete). Through comparison we can begin to move from opacity – if not to transparency, at least to translucency – with shapes and colours becoming visible to the outsider. To be able to lead and authentically protect the honour of subject specialisms, an understanding of their comparative natures is vital. In curriculum theory we can find the ideas and language to give form to the comparisons and analysis that can lead us on our way.

The temptation, outlined in Section 1.5, to reductive interpretation, wholesale adoption, and the imposition of generic requirements is fearsome but it must be resisted.

Theory is powerful because it allows us to see beyond the surface, to see patterns and shapes underlying the obvious and directly observable. Knowledge is rich; it exists in layers of meaning and is so much more than a set of specification bullet points or a list of lesson titles. There are currents, branches, strands, and lenses to be understood and explored. In making these hidden things visible, we are empowered to take an ambitious and scholarly approach to curriculum design. Our efforts will take meaningful shape and exemplify progression, and in so doing, induct our students successfully into what Oakeshott called the "great conversations" of our subjects. Theory gives names to abstract entities; it allows us to think with clarity and engage in the key to curriculum thinking: the subject discourse.

We must be on our guard, however. The power of the abstract is prone to mutate into the folly of the generic, if not handled with extreme care. The substance of curriculum theory can only be of use when thoughtfully and discursively applied to subject-specific thinking; if it becomes an accomplice of genericism or is wielded with brute force, at best it will waste time; at worst it will be devastating to the integrity of the subjects and the fidelity of curriculum thinking. It is imperative that the concepts laid out here are not used reductively as whole-school checklists or mandates, but are fed into specialist, integrative, and holistic work within departments.

Engagement in the subject discourse is, as we have said, the only long-term and sustainable route to excellence and depth in curriculum thinking. Developing this engagement can be far from simple. Subject communities are themselves in differing stages of development. Some are so highly developed that the sheer amount of excellent writing and discussion available can be daunting, and knowing where to start can be a significant challenge. Some are almost nascent, with little established body of discourse, or they may be dominated by a paradigm at odds with a powerful knowledge approach,[1] or with a focus on pedagogy but not curriculum. Some discourses are diverse, with not only significant debate but opposing ideologies, and these can be difficult to navigate for the newcomer. Productive engagement with these discourses needs planning and leadership, as outlined in Section 2.3.

In this ongoing curriculum work, senior leaders need sufficient understanding of the types of knowledge in subjects to be able to find out more by reading and making sense of specialist curriculum documents (such as exam board specifications and textbooks), to have discussions with subject leaders, to challenge them, and to guide them, and to critically assess the quality and alignment of external sources supporting the development of the department (such as subject associations, readings, and individual contacts). This understanding must either extend to allow careful judgement on the appropriateness of policies or practices within particular subjects, or to allow a conversation where a subject specialist can explain and justify why such a thing is or is not appropriate to that subject. There is a fine but crucial line to be trodden between distorting the curriculum by imposing generic practices on all subjects and allowing the possibility that subject leaders could justify anything based on the opacity of their subject specialism. Knowledge of knowledge – a theory of curriculum and an understanding of the specialisms – illuminates that line and makes it easier to tread.

Language

Knowledge about knowledge is in demand. Terms like "substantive", "disciplinary" "procedural" and "declarative" abound in education blogs and articles. Being able to see the differences in types of knowledge is indispensable in planning curriculum, as very often the best format for teaching is closely informed by the type of knowledge being taught, and the development of strands across a curriculum will follow structures in the types of knowledge. It's vital that subject curriculum leaders understand the differences between the types of knowledge in their subject, in order to plan progression and pedagogy and develop understanding of both within their departments.

What subject specialists actually call these aspects of their curriculum work matters less. Senior leaders of curriculum must be able to identify these features by their characteristics, not by the labels they are given. A scheme of work with a dedicated column headed "disciplinary knowledge" does not guarantee a curriculum with strong planning for disciplinary knowledge: it is entirely possible to use a wealth of curriculum terminology and still have very poor curricular thinking. Specialist language must be seen as a means to an end, and not an end in itself, where the end (albeit never actually ending) is deep engagement with the subject matter and its manifestations in curriculum.

An inclination towards the interrogative rather than the imperative or declarative, to question rather than to instruct or tell, and to welcome discussion and challenge from subject specialists, is so often the most effective approach for embedding and developing use of curriculum theory, and engagement with subject specialist discourse.

The questions at the end of this and every other chapter in this book can be used in this way, with the reminder that nothing will apply everywhere and a caution against analysis-reduction creep. These discussions must be seen as part of the discourse, and as a dialectic where development is iterative and never-ending. In building a successful culture of curriculum, discursive conversations such as those flowing from the questions suggested throughout this book can serve both to promote subject-specific and deep-level thinking, and to develop an expectation of challenge and integrity from interlocutors on both sides. It is necessary both for specialists to be supported in ongoing curriculum exploration, applying theory and engagement in specialist discourse, and for non-specialist leaders to be able to support their own developing understanding by inviting challenge and explication of the nuances of the specialisms. Within this dialectic, we can nurture sustained, authentic, and powerful curriculum work, and sustain the discourse. This is the lifeblood of curriculum.

3.1 Disciplines, subjects, and recontextualisation

3.1.1 Disciplines

What is it that makes us human? A large part of the answer to this grand question is "the subject disciplines", and for this reason the leading of curriculum is deeply *human* work. Through the disciplines, we make meaning: we make sense and beauty from the world, we craft expression; we put forward works which allow us to connect with one another and with the universe in all its mystery, depth, and wonder.[2] To experience the fruits of these disciplines, to join the great "conversations of civilisation"[3], to carry that meaning forward and sustain and renew it – these things are the business of schools, and they are wonderful things indeed. The subject disciplines – the institutions of knowledge, the traditions and networks of expertise – are shared and renewed through the school subjects. Music is not just "Wednesday period 4"; it is a creation and tradition, seeking beauty and bringing emotion, reflection, and togetherness to people since the dawn of civilisation. That small section of a child's timeline on a Wednesday period 4 is the connection between this body of understanding, children in the present, and the future into which those children will light their way with the torch of that tradition. Lessons, in this way, are liminal, an interface in time and understanding, and curriculum is both the substance and the pathway of this transaction.

The relationship between school subjects and their related disciplines is not entirely straightforward, and is worth exploring. The concept of "discipline" has been defined as possessing:

- An intellectual history/tradition which is manifested institutionally through higher education

- A body of knowledge founded on core concepts and theories

- A particular object of research or investigation, although this might be shared across disciplines

- Specific terminology and language to define and explain concepts

- Research methods and modes of enquiry according to its specific requirements

- A specific stance towards the nature of reality (i.e. views the world through a particular lens)

- Particular grounds upon which valid truth claims are made/ways of validating knowledge (epistemology)

▪ A group of intellectual followers (academics) who conduct new research in that discipline and bring changes to it over time. [4]

School subjects are clearly linked to these disciplines, but they are not the same thing. In the school subjects, students are introduced to the knowledge and ways of working of the subject disciplines, both so that they may later build on that knowledge should they join the subject disciplines, and for the sake of knowledge itself, and the value we accord to experiencing the world and making meaning through the specialist gazes. The nature of this relationship between subject and discipline is key in curriculum thinking.

3.1.2 Recontextualisation

Sociologist Basil Bernstein characterised the relations of education and disciplines using three distinct but co-dependent "fields" (see Figure 3.1).

1. The field of production, where new knowledge is made. In our wider definition, taking into account the important fact that not all disciplines seek knowledge in any widely accepted understanding of the term, we might say "where new meaning is made". This is largely in universities but also in industry and individuals, practising the disciplines in one way or another as experts and professionals.

2. The field of recontextualisation, where knowledge from the field of production is selected, processed, and prepared, ready for teaching. This field is represented by bodies like the government Department for Education, publishers and authors of textbooks, and the like.

3. The field of reproduction, where students are taught selected knowledge as their foundation in the disciplines – in schools, homeschooling, and so on.[5]

To understand school subjects, therefore, we must first understand the disciplines to which they relate. To understand the disciplines is to gaze on the achievements of the human race, and there is nothing more magnificent. A curator of a gallery cannot paint in the style of all the artists whose work hangs on the walls, but he should understand enough of the work to appreciate and discuss it meaningfully. School leaders can never be experts in all of the specialisms, but we can and must be *appreciators* of them all if we are to lead well. We must seek to understand the purposes, products, functions, structures, and operations

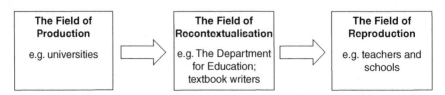

Figure 3.1 Bernstein's three fields

of the disciplines and their recontextualised cousins, the school subjects. Only through this understanding can we authentically challenge, develop, and inspire those most treasured staff, the subject specialists, in their work. No leader of curriculum should struggle to say what the point of geography is, or what technology is all about. We must know the answers to these things, and we must know enough to be able to champion our subjects, to sing their song from the highest tower: we must see all of our subjects as fascinating, glorious, and awe-inspiring, and know why they are so.

Understanding the links and differences between the fields, in other words between school subjects and the disciplines, allows us to reveal some hidden features of the knowledge in school subjects. Table 3.1 shows some suggestions for

Table 3.1 The recontextualisation of school subjects

The Field of Production (disciplines and fields of expertise)	(Recontextualisation)	The Field of Reproduction (school subjects)
Mathematics	→	Mathematics
The sciences (physics, chemistry, biology)	→	Science
Geography; geology; meteorology; climatology; economics; anthropology; sociology	→	Geography
History	→	History
Theology; philosophy; ethics; social sciences; history	→	Religious studies
Modern foreign languages; linguistics	→	Modern foreign languages
Art; history of art	→	Art
Music; history of music	→	Music
English literature; linguistics	→	English and English literature
Sport; sports sciences	→	PE
Design; engineering;	→	Design and technology
Culinary arts; food science	→	Food (usually taught as part of design and technology)
Computer science; information technology	→	Computing

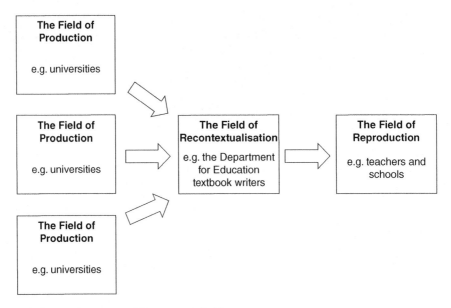

Figure 3.2 An adaptation of Bernstein's fields

how the school subjects, or the fields of reproduction, relate to the disciplines, or the fields of production.

It can be seen from this table that while some subjects are linked with a single discipline, others have more of a composite nature, being recontextualised from a number of disciplines. To return to the fields model, the relationship in these cases is more like that shown in Figure 3.2.

Awareness of the nature and extent of the recontextualisation from field of production to field of reproduction is key for effective curriculum discussions. Such awareness helps to guard against mistaken thinking in curriculum work manifesting as either under-recontextualisation (the curriculum is too close to the discipline to make sense or be appropriate for schoolchildren) or over-recontextualisation (too much of the knowledge or nature of the discipline is lost). In some subjects, recontextualisation is very underdetermined, so that there is significant autonomy as to what can be included in curriculum. Even where recontextualisation is highly specified, it is ongoing, and a live discourse over recontextualisation should be understood to be a pillar of healthy democracy.[6]

Knowledge of recontextualisation then, brings important insights to discussions of curriculum. It allows us to see the place of curriculum in the broader context of knowledge and meaning production and renewal. It can help to reveal the nature of the subject, particularly in the cases of composite subjects, where their heterogeneous features can otherwise bring confusion. We can find direction for our reading and research, particularly where subject discourses are underdeveloped, and learn from the fields of production to inform ambitious curriculum work. And through all of this work, teachers can begin to take their place at the table of recontextualisation, to join the discourse of democracy, in the framing and revising of recontextualisation, so fundamental to a healthy and free society.

3.2 Quests, truth and approval

[E]ach subject is [...] a product and an account of an ongoing truth quest, whether through empirical testing in science, argumentation in philosophy/ history, logic in mathematics or beauty in the arts.

(Counsell, 2018c)

The idea of disciplines as quests is a powerful one. Each discipline is a search for meaning: meaning in different forms, from different starting points, generated in different ways, and these differences are what give us the demarcations of the disciplines. In Section 2.2.2 we outlined some key ideas from philosophers relevant to knowledge and knowers; much of this work is important in our understanding of quests. In practising a discipline, it is *lived-in*: a participant experiences the world through that discipline.[7] What is more, that experience forms part of the self of the participant; their existence is partly constituted by the making of meaning in this way.[8] A discipline's practitioners look out at the world in unique ways; they notice certain types of things, they ask certain types of question, and so on. These dispositions, these characteristic ways-of-looking, and resulting channels-for-meaning, are what we might call the *gaze*[9] of the discipline or subject, though they exist at the level of the individual as well.

Though the quests of each discipline are necessarily unique, some categories can help structure our understanding. We explore these below. Many subjects manifest two or more of these quests, but considering them separately can be illuminating. The nature of quests within a discipline is tightly bound up with conceptions of truth within the discipline and the patterns of development of the body of knowledge, and approval of new knowledge for inclusion in that body. In Section 3.4 we examine some relations of knowledge closely linked to these quests, truth-concepts and methods of approval: we will see that structures of knowledge are, in many ways, manifestations of these orientations and ways of working.

While most disciplines typically combine two or more of the quests below, it is useful to consider each in turn.

3.2.1 Descriptive quests

Many disciplines seek to describe things-in-the-world. However, these disciplines do not merely gather facts, because a collection of facts alone is both too big to make sense of and too shallow to find meaning in. A description always entails an exclusion, a choice, and an integration, in order for it to have value beyond indiscriminate cataloguing. In a descriptive quest, the knower seeks to find facts and to make meaning from them; to distil, interpret, reduce, or generalise. For this reason, though they may covet objectivity, the subject, or knower, is never absent from the descriptive quests. Truth and objectivity however, often tend to be tacitly or explicitly assumed to be, to a greater or lesser degree, attainable and therefore amenable to a shared and single description, notwithstanding the philosophical difficulties with this stance.[10] As such, the rules of logic and empiricism form part of the approval mechanisms for work in these quests, and new knowledge is often added in an integrative model, where new knowledge is either in agreement with incumbent, or replaces incumbent so as to integrate further knowledge. In these ways theories are corroborated or replaced (see Section 3.4.2). Science, mathematics, and some aspects of geography, history, and religious studies have descriptive quests, since they seek to describe what is there-in-the-world, though such description is never entirely or even mostly straightforward or objectivist, as we shall see.

3.2.2 Interpretive quests

Although the role of the knower is to choose what to observe and how to leap from observation to inference, objectivity and single truths are largely assumed to be possible and felt to be desirable in some disciplines far more than in others. The quests of some disciplines are what we might call interpretive. Here, the knower finds meaning from something in the world with an explicit acknowledgment, even championing, of their personal input, and a necessary resultant diversity of thought and absence of consensus. Theology, history, literary criticism, art, and some aspects of geography, all have explicit interpretive aspects to their quests, and do not seek objectivity or single-truth in the way that science and mathematics do. For these quests, approval through reference to logic or empiricism will not suffice, though they are sometimes sought. Instead it falls to the internalist judgement of the subject community to approve work for inclusion within the discipline. New meaning is created in a discursive and accumulative way in these quests: when a new contribution is made to the academic discourse, it often does not usurp work it is in disagreement with, nor prove or corroborate work by its agreement.

3.2.3 Expressive quests

In addition to seeking meaningful descriptions and interpretations of the world, a significant portion of the quests in the disciplines are expressive: producing works that express or create beauty, comment, humour, shock, or some other reaction or experience. Disciplines with expressive quests include art, music, dance, literature, sport and, in part, design. Although these disciplines often incorporate descriptive or interpretive quests alongside the expressive, work produced in these disciplines is usually submitted for approval, not just to the subject community, but to communities of curators, critics, and the interested public. Inclusion for publication, in exhibitions, galleries, concerts and theatres, the responses of critics in the press, and the footfall, feeling and demand from people seeking these experiences, all interact to produce approval of work in these fields.

3.2.4 Solving-producing quests

As humans we seek to understand the world and create expressions, but we also make changes to the physical world around us. We design and produce things, putting objects into-the-world. We solve problems by making things. We make the world we find ourselves in into something different, something we perceive to be better.[11] These "solving-producing" quests are at the heart of disciplines like design, engineering, food, languages, and computing. In these disciplines, we search for a link between the resources available to us, both tangible and abstract, material and concept, and the problems (or opportunities) posed by one or another aspect of life. When we find that link and apply expertise and creativity to the resources available, a product, solution, or program is put into-the-world, to be used for a purpose by people. Although there are institutions such as design museums and awards, and criticism in the form of product reviews, approval of work in these fields is located predominantly with the consumer. If a product works, solves a genuine problem or capitalises effectively on an opportunity in the world, and ultimately pleases the user, then it is approved through demand, and becomes established within the body of work in the field. This democratisation of approval in these disciplines is perhaps one reason why they have not been considered as existing on the same plane as the sciences, arts, and humanities, but as we shall see in Chapter 4, these subjects have challenging and sophisticated bodies of knowledge, and comfortably meet most, if not all of most, if not all of our criteria for disciplines above.

It is the case of course that the world of human culture is complex, layered, and dialectic. Each discipline, dealing with its different objects and ways of operating, is necessarily characterised by its own unique mix of quests, truth-status, and methods of approval; as we explore the details of each of these, we can hope to come closer to the true nature of our disciplines and school subjects.

3.3 Categories of knowledge

Knowledge exists in a non-physical realm, but it shares some illuminating similarities with physical matter. Knowledge comes in different types, like different materials. These types have their own properties, and can be handled more effectively when we understand those properties, and can give names to them. Subjects as wholes can be better understood when the nature of the knowledge within them is brought to light. Work on curriculum is, after all, work on knowledge, and just as the architect builds well with an understanding of her materials, so curriculum work is fed by an understanding of the knowledge being dealt with.

3.3.1 Substantive and disciplinary knowledge

We have said that what disciplines – and therefore school subjects – do is to make meaning in the world, in the shared experience of Husserl's *Lebenswelt*. The type of meaning made by each discipline is a complex product of its quest and its relationship to the world and the knower. Many disciplines produce work that most people would comfortably call knowledge (mathematics, the sciences, and geography, for example) while for other disciplines their contributions sit outside of what we generally group under that term. The contributions of artists, writers, and composers are perhaps more appropriately termed "the body of work" or similar, but there is no question that this work puts meaning into the world just as much as those more obviously knowledge-producing subjects.

Knowledge of the meaning made by a discipline then, can be termed "substantive knowledge": the claims and works put forward and developed by the great contributors in the disciplines over time. It is the understandings and pieces; the canon; the body of work that is considered worth studying.

Disciplinary knowledge, in contrast, can be understood as knowledge of how participation in a discipline or subject allows us to create meaning. Some subjects, as we have seen, have a highly empiricist way of producing knowledge; others do not. Some subjects have an overtly interpretivist approach, where the involvement of the scholar in the production of knowledge is a significant and acknowledged factor in the nature of the contribution; in others the identity of the scholar has less prominence. How ideas are presented and developed, as figures, statements, pieces, products and essays, all form part of the disciplinary code. In teaching disciplinary knowledge and laying out these codes, students can be inducted into the discipline, and experience the world through these multiple and diverse lenses.

The distinction between substantive and disciplinary knowledge is important for several reasons. Young's conception of curriculum in Future 3 (see Section 2.2.1) rests on two pillars: powerful knowledge in the sense of best knowledge within a discipline, and an awareness of the constructed and ongoing nature of that knowledge as the result of a community and discourse: not "knowledge-from-on-high", fixed and closed, as was the case with Future 1 curriculum. Thus, the quality of knowledge content in curriculum, and the knowledge of how such knowledge is produced – substantive and disciplinary knowledge respectively – are both givers-of-power and must be understood and planned for explicitly. Both a sophisticated knowledge of the substance of the subjects, and an understanding of how they work are needed for students to experience the world in all the richness of meaning we have, and to be able to join the ranks of specialists in further study.

For specialists working on curriculum, the work can feel disjointed and frustrating if substantive and disciplinary strands are not identified and understood. To jump from the elegance of mechanics to the pragmatism of experimentation in the planning of science curriculum can feel like a step down, a tiresome chore. Similarly teaching students how to analyse poetry and the appreciation of a poem as a work of art are often unhelpfully conflated. Understanding the curriculum as having substantive and disciplinary strands allows us to see that this latter work may not always be elegant but it is noble. The empirical method in science has been fought for, over hundreds of years by brave pioneers, some of whom lost their lives because they insisted that to look upon the world as it is, and not as we wish it to be, should be a standard of knowledge-making. In history, the reverse is often true. The elegance and sophistication of the subject is most manifest when the development of disciplinary work is explicitly taught and developed in students, lifting curriculum beyond what can feel like a string of substantive claims, "one damn thing after another".[12] Though of course, the disciplinary in history is utterly contingent upon a wealth of substantive knowledge. In naming strands in this way we can make sense of our experience of knowledge behaving differently in curriculum, and in doing so bring clearer thinking and more rewarding curriculum work.

If substantive and disciplinary strands are not clearly identified, one or the other runs the risk of being overlooked in curriculum work. In some subjects, such as history, there is an essential reciprocal relationship between the two strands, where it is only possible for understanding to be reached in one strand through building on the other; for this building to be done effectively, the strands must be seen clearly. In being able to name these strands, teachers working on curriculum are able to engage in discourse of a precise and sophisticated nature, and through this develop excellence in their curriculum thinking and execution.

The balance and interplay of the substantive and disciplinary strands, the amount of insight that can be gained from analysis of a subject using those strands, and the relevance for school subjects, are diverse across the subjects. In some subjects, other models may prove more useful. It is therefore imperative – as we have said already, and will say again before the end – that each subject is treated as unique: substantive and disciplinary knowledge should be discussed where it is appropriate, and other models of knowledge must be used elsewhere.

3.3.2 Declarative, non-declarative, and motor knowledge

Both philosophers[13] and cognitive scientists[14] posit a distinction between declarative knowledge, or *knowing-that*, and non-declarative knowledge, or *knowing-how*. These types of knowledge have also variously been called propositional or statement knowledge, and procedural and process knowledge respectively.[15] These are useful distinctions to make, and we see knowledge from both categories across the subjects.

Declarative knowledge might be characterised as articulatable knowledge; things-about-the-world such as facts, ideas, opinions, and imaginings. These exist as statements and links between the statements. Declarative knowledge occupies both substantive and disciplinary strands in varying proportions across the subjects.

In non-declarative, or procedural knowledge, we are able to do something, to carry out a process. Often, we struggle to articulate how we do this, and this points to the often tacit nature of procedural knowledge. In solving problems, analysing texts, and composing arguments, we draw on procedural knowledge to take us beyond the declarative components that we bring together in this work. We find non-declarative knowledge in both substantive and disciplinary strands, and in different proportions across our subjects. In subjects with a practical element, physical skill falls under the non-declarative category of knowledge, and is often described by cognitive scientists as motor knowledge. For these subjects the practical–theory distinction for knowledge is often useful, provided the components of those two categories are carefully and ambitiously analysed and mapped.

These categories of knowledge within a discipline bring implications for sequencing, mapping for progression, teaching, and student work, and should thus be a principal consideration in curriculum thinking. Within each subject we find specialist categories of knowledge in addition to those described here; we shall explore some of these in Chapter 4 when we consider each subject in turn.

3.3.3 Ways of looking or "gazes"

Each subject has its own lens or set of lenses to turn on the world, its own "gaze", to use the sociologists' terminology. Noticing the light, noticing composition, seeking explanations, seeing wholes, seeing parts, seeking the right answer, accommodating multiple interpretations, relating to other works in the field such as writers in the same genre, are all ways of looking and there are many, many more. These gazes are often tacit for practitioners of a subject but they are worth making explicit in curriculum thinking. In fact, it is crucial that we do. If we fail to make the implicit explicit we will guarantee that many students will fail to understand how to make meaning in our subjects and will not be fully inducted into the ongoing cultural discourse. Although some students may come to experience a particular "gaze" through incidental osmotic process, this cannot be left to chance. There are certainly some experiential elements of gaze and living – in a subject which must remain impossible to fully articulate, emergent and not amenable to explicit verbalisations – but these should be what remains after a concerted effort, and not an oversized mass created by a deficit in thinking. The gaze of the subject, once explicated in curriculum thinking, can be reflected in the stories, narrative, examples, and tasks built into the working curriculum, and indeed in the intentional exclusion of anachronisms that would weaken the disciplinary gaze: in fidelity to the discipline, the gaze of the specialist is both modelled and developed. Thus, we might avoid cartoons, contemporary icons, and ethical questions in history curricula, for example, since these things are ahistorical and are enemies of the historian's gaze.

3.3.4 The inclusion and exclusion of knowledge

Time is finite, and so curriculum can never include all the knowledge, or even anything close to all the knowledge, in the field. As such, curriculum is necessarily exclusive: decisions must be made as to the knowledge that is included and that which is excluded. All knowledge in curriculum is therefore an opportunity cost, and the decisions over which knowledge to include must therefore rest on some kind of value judgment between areas of knowledge. For some subjects this is relatively straightforward; there is broad agreement in the subject communities around what should be taught at school, usually because of features of the structure of knowledge and progression within the subject, as in the cases of maths, science, and languages. These subjects tend to have tightly defined requirements in national curricula and exam specifications, so there is usually not a great deal for curriculum writers in schools to have to decide upon with regard to inclusion and exclusion of knowledge.

In other subjects however there is little or no such agreement. Subjects with a more interpretive nature and/or a flattish ontology (see Sections 3.3.2 and 3.5.1) such as history, religious studies, English or art, often have much less definition in the official requirements and much more freedom to choose in the question of "which knowledge?" This under-determinism in the documentation is deliberate, of course, and reflects the fact that there is almost certainly no single correct answer to this question, though there are certainly stronger and weaker answers. In the multiplicity of people working on curriculum in these areas we have a multiplicity of knowers and interpretations; we should expect debate and diversity of responses to the question of "which knowledge" and welcome the ongoing nature of this discourse. This is not to say that these debates do not and should not exist for those more highly determined subjects as well, but those debates are typically both less diverse and less prolific. As we have already seen in Section 2.1.3, the subject of recontextualisation is fundamental to democracy, and the empowerment of teachers to join that debate is something we must seek and develop through our curriculum work.

An important tool of analysis here is Michael Fordham's conception of independent necessity vs collective sufficiency.[16] Fordham observes that to ask simply what parts should be included in a curriculum represents a category error, in that a curriculum is more than its parts and so cannot be judged solely on those terms. Thus, we might not be able to point to any particular item in a curriculum and state that it is essential, but taken as a whole, a group of items can represent a good curriculum: collective sufficiency obtains, or perhaps emerges, from the group. It follows too that we must be careful to avoid simplistic analysis of knowledge and curriculum, and ask about the functions of groups as well as individual pieces of knowledge, and the relations between parts and wholes. In leading curriculum, instead of saying:

"Justify the inclusion of each piece of knowledge in your curriculum"

we would often do better to ask

"How do these parts together mean that the student leaves with a good understanding?"

In Section 3.4.4 below we will explore this idea further in the study of relations of knowledge.

3.4 Relations of knowledge

The bodies of knowledge in the disciplines – the substantive claims and the meaning they put into the world, as well as the disciplinary methods and codes involved in doing so – exist in *relations*. Knowledge within disciplines is grouped into areas or sections; ideas are linked to other ideas, and the natures of these links and the structures they create are significant. The differences in the subjects, in the types of meaning that we make from them, and the ways they behave, are partly due to their different structures of relations. These structures are reflected (though often tacitly) in the schemata of specialists, and understanding them can inform the planning of the building of schemata, in other words, curriculum work.

These patterns of knowledge in a subject can reflect many and diverse aspects of the discipline: the objects of study, the meanings made about and through them, the ways in which the discipline operates in generating new meaning, and the ways the knowledge relates in sense-making or learning. These structures can feel almost tangible when one is dealing with them, finding one's way around the knowledge in a subject, exploring its mountains, planes, and archipelagos, and their natures should be manifest in curriculum thinking. Basil Bernstein's work[17] has been seminal in this analysis, but further work is needed. It is common for words like "hierarchical" and "cumulative" to be used in relation to curriculum, but these have been used variously to describe

- the organisation of the body of knowledge

- the level of determinism of the links

- the disciplinary patterns of knowledge production, and

- the principles of progression through the subject.

Table 3.2 Relations of knowledge

Plane of relations	Definition	Spectrum end 1	Examples	Spectrum end 2	Examples
Ontological architecture/ ontology	The relations between the objects of study in levels of fundamentalness	Taller	Mathematics, science	Flatter	English literature, history
Integration of knowledge	The relations between the objects of study in the determinism of the links	Stronger	Mathematics, science, languages, music theory	Weaker	English literature, religious studies
Epistemological patterns	The patterns of knowledge production and knowledge renewal	Unifying	Mathematics, science, physical geography	Discursive/ accumulative	Art, history, English literature, religious studies
Manthanology	The relations in how components should be ordered for understanding	Necessity	Mathematics, science, languages, music theory	Sufficiency	History, English literature

Though all of these things are linked, they are not the same, and there are important curricular implications from each. Karl Maton's Legitimation Code Theory (LCT)[18] and others' work in this research programme have provided important insights into these relations, and the ideas in this section draw heavily on that work.

These four different types of knowledge relations can be visualised as planes, or spectra. These planes, and the types of structures that can occupy them, are summarised in Table 3.2, and explored below.

Following Maton,[19] these are conceived of as spectra rather than binaries, with subjects falling somewhere along a continuum rather than being one extreme or another.

Let us consider each of these planes in turn.

3.4.1 Ontological architecture

We have seen how the fundamental nature of knowledge can be either declarative or non-declarative, and how its role in a subject can be either substantive or disciplinary, or practical and theoretical, and so on, but at the level of the specialist, subject knowledge is often grouped together in areas of similarity or relation. Thus, it is useful to talk about knowledge of topics, concepts, and themes within the subjects, while the knowledge within these areas may be diverse in its makeup.

Within and between these groups, pieces of knowledge are linked. The number and significance of these links has been termed *semantic density* in LCT[20] and this is an important property of knowledge in a subject. Emergent from these pieces of knowledge and the links between them are patterns of knowledge, which we shall consider in this section.

These links are critical to the meaning held in the knowledge of a subject: they allow the knower to see patterns, make connections, draw pieces together, and make new meaning from the world. For example, in solving a geometry problem, we might draw on knowledge of interior angles of polygons, related knowledge of how to mark up a diagram to show these angles, an ability to recognise triangles, and a related knowledge of trigonometry, in order to come to a solution. The navigation of knowledge in memory and the resulting ability to *think* are as contingent on these links between pieces of knowledge as they are on the pieces themselves.[21] Making new meaning, solving problems, and creative thinking – indeed mental productions of any kind – are an expression of movement through schemata.

In many of our subjects, the objects of study are linked by relationships that are themselves the objects of study. A is explained by B, C is composed of D, or E causes F; these objects, explanations and compositions may be termed the ontology of the subject. The architectures of these ontologies within subjects range from tall to flat, as a reflection of the number of levels of hierarchy, of abstraction, composition, or explanation. Where subjects have many levels, such as in mathematics or science, we can describe a tall ontology. Where there are fewer levels, such as in history or English, we find a flatter ontology, though never completely flat, since all disciplines involve theory, which always creates an abstraction of meaning. Note that this is not to say that there is *less* theory in a flatter ontology than in a taller one, but that there is not the highly layered relationship between areas of theory. Thus in English we might have particulars of a text on one ontological level, themes such as responsibility and atavism at another, knowledge of context such as Victorian life at another, and knowledge of literary devices at another. These are all fascinating and important, but apart from possibly the particulars of the text being in one sense more concrete and specific, it is not clear which area of knowledge here is more fundamental than another. Compare this with the ontology of science, where the properties of a material are explained by the arrangement of its molecules, which is explained by its composite atoms, which is explained by the structure of those atoms, and so on. The layering here is clear, and we see a 'tall' architecture of ontology. Articulating these differences in architecture allows us to put our finger on some of the differences between the subjects that we often sense but can't define; and they are useful to the specialist since it is the links themselves that embody so much of the expert's understanding of a field, and which are so often missed in curriculum planning as they are rendered invisible by the *curse of knowledge*.[22]

Another concept from LCT which is useful here is that of *semantic gravity*. For subjects where the abstract or fundamental is king, and details of examples are less important, such as in science and mathematics, we can use the term "low semantic gravity," since the knowledge floats and transcends the examples and the instances. For subjects such as geography and history, where the details of specifics and the concrete are key, we can use the term "moderate semantic gravity," as the knowledge in these context-dependent areas is pulled down to the contexts, just as masses are pulled to Earth. Note that "high semantic gravity" is not used here, since concepts and abstract ideas are also of importance in these disciplines. Domains with very high semantic gravity would not be disciplines at all, since they would be devoid of theory: cataloguing of data, such as might be found in an old-fashioned telephone directory, is a more appropriate contender for consistently high semantic gravity. Clarity on the levels of semantic gravity in a subject can help us to avoid faux-pas like pushing for generalisations where they are not appropriate, such as in history; and can prompt emphasis on them where they are powerful, such as in science.

3.4.2 Integration

In subjects such as maths, science, languages and music theory, we typically find a tightly defined "grammar" of the knowledge, with universal and precise definitions, agreed and shared units and lexicon, and consistent rules for application of concepts and execution of procedures. In other subjects, these things are often less fixed, and there are several ways of linking knowledge and making meaning, with no universal agreement. These properties of stronger or weaker *integration of knowledge* are often reflected in the types of questions and answers we find in the subjects,[23] since those with tight grammars and strong integration tend to have right-or-wrong answers, while in those with more flexible grammars and weaker integration there is less determinism in the relationships between areas. In these subjects, many responses and interpretations are often possible, and questions are typically more open, with responses marked against a rubric rather than a tightly defined mark scheme.

A common perception is often that taller ontologies or stronger integrations of knowledge are indicators of subjects that are either purer, better, harder, or all three. This is a mistake. Ontological structures and integrations of knowledge, tall or flat, strong or weak, are simply *there in the world*, in one sense or another.[24] These properties are not choices by knowers, or virtues or vices of an object of study. In studying a tall domain like physics or mathematics, we find a tall ontology, and good for us. If we study a different domain, such as anything to do with human behaviour, or anything expressive, we will likely find a flatter ontological architecture, and weaker integrations, because that is the nature of those domains, or at least the meaning made within those domains. This is not to say that such domains are not complex, challenging, conceptual or worthy. It is simply the case that the ideas do not exist with the same ascending relations and tight integrations in the worlds of these subjects. The subjects are incommensurable: it does not make sense to try to compare these properties to see which is better, because such properties are functions of the objects of study, and are tied to them.

3.4.3 Epistemological patterns

The methods used to discover or create new meaning, *viz* the operations of the discipline, create a structure in what we might call the epistemological plane: the plane of knowledge production. There are often significant similarities here with ontological architectures; we might expect our ways of making meaning to be shaped by the things being studied, just as roads tend to reflect the topology of a country, but they are not the same thing. "The map is not the territory", as Alfred Korzybski tells us.[25] Particularly when the role of other knowers, in their interpretation or expression, is itself an object of study, as in history, literature or music, *ways of knowing* themselves cause links of meaning between knowledge in the discipline, and we find schools of thought, movements, themes and so on. In mathematics and science, by contrast, we find highly unifying epistemological structures, where new meaning is made and added to the discipline either by fitting neatly into pre-existing principles or (in revolutions)[26] by replacing earlier unifying principles with new and more powerful ones. Thus, we get tidy and tall tree-like epistemological structures in mathematics and science, where new meaning is made on the many levels of the ontology, and is fitted in in agreement with more fundamental levels, with no significant conflicts. And in subjects where the role of the knower is more prominent, where the nature of the objects of study means calculations or empiricism are not productive ways of creating meaning, we find the development of knowledge follows a non-linear, discursive, additive, and accumulative pattern, such as in history, art, and religious studies.

An interesting manifestation of these differences is that in subjects where epistemological patterns are highly unifying, most scholarship from the field of production is both difficult to access for school students of the subject, and seldom relevant in terms of contributing to the recontextualised curriculum. For subjects with an accumulative or discursive epistemology, in contrast, such scholarship is often both accessible and valuable in curricular terms, and can be a powerful inclusion in curriculum.

As has already been noted, epistemological structures closely mirror the ontological – however it is worth understanding them separately, as different implications arise from each. While ontology can inform a structure we seek to build through our curriculum, epistemological structure shows us something that might inform what we teach students about the ways of working within a subject, and it helps to shed light on why the types of activity in curricula are different: as meaning is renewed in lessons, with students being inducted into the methods, they might solve problems by integrating into tight grammars, as in maths and science, or they might analyse contributions and then produce their own discursive work, as in English and history, for example.

3.4.4 Manthanology

Ontology and epistemology are taken from the Greek for *being* and *knowing* respectively. It is the case that structures arise in subjects, beyond being and knowing, in a plane of *learning*. While being and knowing are present participles, they have little in the way of temporal overtones: they exist in time but not acutely on a timeline. Learning, however, is highly temporal, with stages, development, remembering, and culminating all happening across a distinct axis, a narrative arc. This gives rise to relations in knowledge in disciplines that cannot be accurately articulated through either ontological or epistemological structures or relations. There are some things that must be learned first – and the reasons for this are not systematic. Sometimes a cause should be learned before an effect – but at other times the reverse can be true. Sometimes a part must be learned before the whole – but not always. Sometimes it doesn't matter what is learned first, and sometimes there are arguments either way. This cognitive directionality (or its absence) of knowledge within a subject – its property of being one-way, or two-way, or contestable-way – creates a structure in the knowledge that must be attended to.

Since the Greek for learning is *manthano*, we shall call this the *manthanological* plane. The manthanological directionality of most subjects is diverse, with some areas being highly directional, with contingency of one item upon the security of another, and other areas adirectional, being amenable to teaching in one order as much as another. In fact at times we encounter manthanological paradoxes, where knowledge could be significantly integrated and therefore simplified, and made more sense of, by an idea that nevertheless needs to be taught later, either because it is intrinsically too challenging or because it relies on other component knowledge yet to be taught. For example, in science the behaviour of electric circuits could be clearly and simply understood using Maxwell's equations, but because these are beyond the scope of secondary mathematics in the UK at present, this unifying and simplifying piece of knowledge is kept back, and the electricity curriculum is initially less well integrated than it will become for students who pursue further study.

In Section 3.3.4 we saw how knowledge in curriculum can be analysed according to independent necessity versus collective sufficiency. The balance of these qualities is largely a reflection of the integration of knowledge in a subject, and has implications for the manthanology of a subject. In subjects with strong integrations, such as maths and languages, there are specific components that must be mastered in order to access a particular piece of new knowledge, and we can identify a *manthanology of necessity*. In subjects with weaker integrations, it is not the case that anything can be taught in any order; nevertheless there are a number of ways of building readiness for specific new learning: we can see this as a *manthanology of sufficiency*.[27]

It is important to see these four planes of relations as separate, although of course there are overlaps and reflections between the planes. These relations inform many further aspects of curriculum thinking, explored elsewhere in this book. The ontological architecture of a subject is useful in the specifying and organising of the knowledge we want to build in a curriculum (Chapter 5); while the strength of its integration helps us to characterise the subjects with accuracy (Section 3.2), and to choose appropriate models of work and assessment (Chapter 5 and Section 3.5 respectively). The epistemological patterns help to explicate the disciplinary nature of the subject (Section 3.3.1), and the manthanological structure gives us a framework for thinking about progression and sequencing (Sections 3.5 and 3.6). Analysis of subjects along these planes supports clear vision of components and characters of the subjects, and protection of the integrity of the specialisms.

3.4.5 Core and hinterland

In addition to the structures and planes described above, there are important relations in the relative roles and prominences of pieces of knowledge within a subject. We might add another dimension to our visualisations, and posit a foreground and background. Across this axis we can position what have been called *core* and *hinterland* knowledge, though more accurately yet another dimension would be needed to reflect the fact that the relative foregrounding of knowledge can change over time in curriculum, as earlier core can become later hinterland. For example, early science curriculum might have as core knowledge a description of the characteristics and key features of the classes of animalia; later on when interdependence and trophic levels are core knowledge, the residual knowledge of that earlier core gives a depth and meaning to the discussions of feeding relationships, habitats, and the like, that would be absent without that hinterland built previously as core. In core knowledge, we find the headlines, the key points, the knowledge-at-hand. In the hinterland resides the details, the richness, the backdrop which gives shape, depth, and placement to the core. Neither is complete without the other, and it is partly in these relations that meaning is held in a subject. The quality of a curriculum is built as much by its background details as by its headlines, and to neglect either is to disservice the discipline, and to emaciate the subject.

> The act of reading the full novel is like the hinterland. However much pupils might be advised to study or create distillations, commentaries and

plot summaries, however much these become decent proxies for (and aids towards) the sort of thing that stays in our heads after we've read the novel, to bypass reading the novel altogether would be vandalism. [28]

The extent and significance of the relations of knowledge in a subject should point us to the crucial importance of considering curriculum *as a whole* before beginning work on any of its parts. Though ultimately curriculum must be knowledge structured over time, the planning of this must be in response to the shape of, and relations within, the final desired outcome: the sophisticated set of knowledge and connections that comprises the body of the discipline and its knowledge.

3.5 Progression

3.5.1 "The curriculum as the progression model"

What does it mean to get better at a subject? The ultimate aim of curriculum must be to structure a path, a movement through knowledge in time, where travel leads to acquisition and understanding, to seeing the world in a new way. This means that the answers to this deceptively simple question are key to curriculum work.

For some time, much of the thinking about progression within subjects was bound up with the faulty "level descriptors" model, or "Bloom's taxonomy". Many schools and teachers have now mercifully been freed from these unhelpful and distortionary diktats, but to replace them with something meaningful and true to one's subject requires careful thought, *to wit*, a progression model.

"The curriculum as the progression model"[29] is a powerful and liberating idea: if students are learning (and remembering) more of the curriculum, they are making progress. This concept frees us from faulty imaginings about progress and places the locus of the progression model firmly in the curriculum itself. The curriculum as the progression model tells us nothing about progression, other than where we should look to find its definitions, and rightly so, since progression is utterly bound up with specialist knowledge and cannot be meaningfully described in generic terms. A curriculum must be built for progression, then, if it is to serve well as our progression model. But what does that mean? What does developing a curriculum for progression look like?

3.5.2 Progression in a curriculum

To get at the meat of these questions we should begin at the end, and ask what kind of things we wish to see in a student at the end of their study of an exceptional curriculum:

- What should they *know*?

- What should they be able to *do*?

- What sort of questions should they be able to answer?

- How should they be able to see and interpret the world?

- What should they be able to bring with them in readiness for the next stage of study, should they pursue that route?

If they are well-designed, final assessments such as examinations can often give us a useful window onto discussion of these end-points, but the call to resist reductivism should ever sound in our ears. We must remember that these examinations are a measurement of the knowledge – a proxy – and not the knowledge itself.

The sorts of answers we come to for the question "What does it mean to get better at this subject?" will reflect the subject under consideration: Will students be able to solve lots of hard problems? Write excellent essays about a range of topics? Be able to answer lots of this or that type of question? Produce a piece that is good for such-and-such specified reasons? And so on.

A common mistake here is to conflate so-called "assessment objectives" with curricular objects. It is important to clear this up entirely. From curriculum, knowledge is learned, or at least, that should be our intention. An assessment samples the student, and measures things that can be measured, in order to make inferences about what has taken place in the student. Assessments are constructed in order to measure and allow inferences to be made. Subjects tend to follow either the difficulty or quality model (or a mixture of the two).[30] Where subjects fit the difficulty model, such as mathematics and science, questions are answered and the response is right or wrong. In product-model subjects such as art and English, pieces of work such as paintings or essays are marked according to a rubric set up along criteria.

Assessment objectives are used both to structure rubrics for product-model assessment, and to distribute questions for difficulty-models, but these are just attempts at heuristics that have been created in order to facilitate a measurement being taken of something that is difficult to measure. They are like the camera used to capture the winner of a race. Athletes should not be concerned with this camera while they are running, they should be concerned with running. Similarly, in curriculum the methods of assessment should not be the starting point for curriculum content: such conflation is a category error and damaging to curriculum work. A focus on assessment objectives when working on curriculum inevitably leads to the omission of the explicit teaching and practice of the component parts that go into making a successful outcome, since these are not highlighted in mark schemes.

This is not to say that the difficulty-model and quality-model are not themselves useful categories for curriculum, since they can give clarity of thought to the type of work set and the type of feedback, though an interesting detail is that often components of product-model can be effectively taught within a difficulty-model. For example, in learning how to write essays, students may study a number of sentence and grammatical exercises, as well as perhaps some substantive propositions about a text – all of which can take a right-or-wrong format – before synthesising these components into essay construction.

The next step is to consider the journey to these final destinations, and to remember the advice from Christine Counsell, paraphrasing Daisy Christodoulou, that, "most of the time, the final accomplishment does not resemble the means of its nurture."[31] Identifying the components of final success – particularly where the final success is a process drawing on tacit knowledge and unconscious abilities – is challenging, but vital to curriculum work. One of the hallmarks of excellent curricular thinking and indeed classroom teaching is the analysis of the composite nature of expert work in the subject, the identification of the components of the composite whole, the careful sequencing, instruction, and practising of these components, and the bringing of them together, to allow students to travel their path with success. Fortunately, such thinking forms the subject of growing discussion in the subject discourses.[32]

The acquisition of these components of success, then, and an increasing ability to draw upon them and to draw them together, are the general substance of a progression model. The excavation of these components, and the mapping of them for logical sequentialism and cognitive ascension, are vital curriculum work for the subject specialist and the wider subject discourse. Broadly speaking, these components might fall into the following categories:

- Knowing more pieces of declarative knowledge

- Knowing more (declarative) links between pieces of knowledge

- Knowing more components of processes and more processes

- Increasing motor knowledge – increasing physical ability or skill

- Knowing more examples of applications or manifestations of declarative knowledge

- Knowing more examples of applications of processes

And all of these result in:

- Being able to correctly answer more questions and harder questions

- Being able to produce pieces of work of a higher standard

The nature of progression within a subject occupies the interface between knowledge, cognition, and measurement, all of which have significant bodies of theory behind them and which require careful thought and analysis to draw together. Together with an understanding of the categories and relations of knowledge within a subject, progression is the final component that will feed into one of the grand tasks of curriculum: sequencing, and the subject of our next section.

3.6 Knowledge over time: sequencing of curriculum

3.6.1 An introduction to sequencing

Up to this point we have largely considered knowledge out-of-time. We have studied the nature of the end product, the goal of teaching a subject, and the parts that might make up that whole. It is time now to turn to the business of sequencing, since learning happens over time, and time is narrow, successive, and linear.

The order in which things are taught matters. Building knowledge, like building anything else, needs ground laying, strong foundations, and supporting structures. This is perhaps an obvious truth, but the sequencing of curriculum is far from facile, as we shall see.

Before undertaking any sequencing work, an understanding of the nature, structure, and components of knowledge and the exercises needed to develop success, as we have explored in the previous sections, is required. Sequencing of curriculum does not require (and should sometimes explicitly avoid) emulating the ontological structure of knowledge in the subject – for example, it can often be undesirable to begin with all of the most fundamental principles – but as the ultimate goal is the creation of this knowledge structure in the memory of the student, then it should be considered in the development of sequence. An understanding of all of the pieces that are components of sophisticated knowledge and ability in a student must be clear before planning, so that those pieces can be explicitly mapped and taught in turn before being brought together. The differences between the final product and the means of its nurture must be well understood in order for effective development of the student and their successful journey along the curriculum path. And the natures, roles, and significances of the various strands of knowledge within a subject must be seen clearly in order to plan well-balanced curriculum, giving proper treatment to all those strands.

Curriculum, ultimately, is (metaphorically) a narrative, a journey, and a conversation. Not just "one damn thing after another,"[33] but a development of meaning over time. Our overarching approach, then, should at times be that of the narrator: to present things in an order that makes sense, to allow things to unfold meaningfully, to deliberately craft readiness[34] for the things still to come. A curriculum should be crafted as a whole, so that it has coherence: knowledge should build and speak to other knowledge across the curriculum in a thorough and orderly way. Much of this is intuitive, if we give ourselves time to think about it. We tend to group things together in topics or units. Some units make sense to go before others, and some after. Some make sense to follow on from each other, since they are related or conceptually proximal.

The devil, as he so often is, is in the detail. Knowledge, as we have seen, exists in different categories, strands, components, relations, and forms. Units are not homogeneous in the types of knowledge they comprise. They encompass facts, procedures, links, components, and composites. The broad components of success that we discussed in Section 3.5 are unlikely to sit within single units or be tied to them, but rather to float or be tied down to several substantive areas. These components must be sequenced for meaning too, but the standard model of units cannot cover this sequencing implicitly.

We might conceive then, of central curriculum spines: units crystallised from principles or themes, through which the curriculum is organised and broad narrative developed. Units might be conceptual, temporal, spatial, and so on, and from their names and order, allow meaning to unfold. Around, within, through and across these central spines must attend the components and strands that do not obviously structure the sequencing in a primary way, but are nonetheless crucial to the curriculum, like satellites orbiting the planetary masses of our subject disciplines.

For some subjects, enquiry questions can provide a scholarly way to largely unite spines and satellites, and substantive and disciplinary knowledge. There is a sophisticated body of subject-specific work on the use of enquiry questions in subjects such as history and geography, and in some other subjects, project-type units can structure theory and practical work in a meaningful way.

Several principles can inform our considerations of spines, satellites, enquiry questions and projects in sequencing curriculum: manthanology, narrative, semantic waving, interweaving, and synthesis. Let us explore each of these in turn.

3.6.2 Manthanology

In Section 3.4.4 we saw how the manthanology of a subject reflects the contingencies of parts of curriculum on previously mastered knowledge. We saw that in some subjects there is a manthanology of necessity, where certain, specifiable components must be taught before particular new knowledge is mastered, while in others there is a manthanology of sufficiency, where there are a number of possible sets of prior knowledge that can prepare a student for a new piece of learning. That said, in composite or multi-disciplinary subjects we typically find a corresponding diversity of manthanologies. The following questions must be asked in planning curriculum:

- What knowledge is independently necessary in order to access later knowledge?
- What knowledge is cumulatively sufficient?
- Where is the order crucial?
- Where is there flexibility?

The challenge here often lies in identifying the components of this required knowledge, and the means of its nurture – things that are often difficult to see through the veil of expertise – but this is important work, and as with all these things is made easier through engagement in the subject discourse.

3.6.3 Narrative

In building knowledge over time we are both engaging students in cognitive activity and seeking for them to build long-lasting cognitive structures of their own. The "privileged status of stories"[35] in psychology points us to our second principle of sequencing: narrative, and its power to engage cognition and memory. Where curriculum unfolds, marches, leads, and ushers, like a story being told, meaning and memory are predisposed to being made. Some things make sense before other things, some things lead in nicely, some things provide useful context, contrast, and highlights, and the instinct for a good story, as much as an analytical approach to drama and narrative arc, must play a part in the art of curriculum-building. Of course, some subjects have a much more pronounced quality of narrative in the obvious sense, but in all subjects we can consider qualities such as foreshadowing, unfolding, revealing, and resolution.

The curriculum must be seen as a whole, made of parts which play roles across time. Christine Counsell articulates these roles thus:

> Each bit of a curriculum is always doing a job in making the next stage possible (**a proximal function**) but it is also doing an enduring job (**an ultimate function**) which might come into its own later, sometimes much later.[36]

Thus the curriculum must be considered simultaneously in its entirety and in its details if it is to have the most meaning for students, so that each part supports the others both immediately near it and more distantly down the timeline. As narrative unfolds over multiple timescales and levels, students can develop rich and three-dimensional understandings, making meaning from the bringing together of these multiple components and competencies, and building powerful and lasting schemata from their experiences.

3.6.4 Semantic waving

The concept of semantic waving comes from Karl Maton's Legitimation Code Theory and echoes Siegfried Engelmann's Principles of Instruction. These approaches describe the introduction of material with a concrete, specific, or contextualised example or examples, before describing the more general principle, concept, or idea manifested in the instances first presented. This provides a sort of "cognitive stepping-stone" where students are guided in their understanding of the abstract by being given a model in the material, familiar, or visualisable world on which to build into the more abstract or context-independent plane. From this "crest", students then move to other contexts, material manifestations, or examples, and in doing so explore the power of the principle, the common deep features of situations with differing surface features, and also a particular way of looking in moving beyond that surface to the principles beneath. In this we see the application of the distinction from cognitive science between flexible and inflexible knowledge.[37]

In this model, Pythagoras' theorem would be taught first using a triangle with numbered sides, before generalising to the algebraic formula, and then moving to problems with new triangles, triangles in different orientations, and problems where the triangles themselves must be uncovered, for example.[38] While this waving is often intuitive in curriculum planning, it is equally often overlooked, with curriculum episodes beginning with abstract definitions, or insufficient practice of applications of principles to contexts. However, this waving is not something that ought to be used indiscriminately: the different subjects have different relations between ontological levels, as we saw in Section 3.4.1, and moving from concrete to abstract and back again has a different power in science compared with history, for example. Slavish adherence to the model without regard to the particulars of the subject itself could easily become distorting and problematic.[39] Semantic waving is a useful, if generic idea, and as with all generic ideas it must be used with caution if curriculum work is to be truly authentic.

Over a curriculum, semantic waving might be built in over many timescales. In some places the cycle might be completed in a single lesson; in others it might be over a unit, in other places ideas might be developed across months or years. Concrete particulars might be given as temporary scaffolds or developed for fluency, depending on the requirements of the curriculum in question, before moving to abstraction. In this way the ideas of narrative become intertwined with semantic waving, and we can begin to ask about the unfolding of knowledge in such a way as to allow students to grasp abstract ideas and develop the ability to apply them, within the requisite subject sensitivities as always.

3.6.5 Interweaving[40]

As we have seen, the links between pieces of knowledge are as important as the pieces themselves, and in interweaving a curriculum, components from across the domain are brought together so as to explicate those links, and allow the practice of them. The nature of interweaving may vary across and within subjects. We might see themes reflected across years, for example in English, exploring "the hero" through first the Odyssey, then Romeo and Juliet, then Frankenstein, and finally Macbeth, informed each time through Aristotelian analysis.[41] We might see repeated multiple approaches to areas, for example studying places in geography through tectonics, river landscapes, settlement patterns and industry. Or we might simply see a few sentences in booklets, or a question or two, picking up a place that the current knowledge is linked to previously studied knowledge, and giving an opportunity to think about that link. In these, and in many other ways of sequencing curriculum in order to show links and build strength of association and transfer between areas, we can be said to be interweaving, showing students the full power of the knowledge in the curriculum, and building strong memories of that knowledge and its connections.

3.6.6 Components and bringing-together

We have seen that many of the most challenging aspects of curriculum, the construction of sophisticated essays, the development of high-quality practical projects, and the solving of complex problems, are in fact syntheses of a number of components, which, once identified, can be taught and practised individually, and carefully brought together in order to develop students' composite abilities in these fields. The identification and sequencing of both these components and their bringing-together is our final principle of sequencing, and often the most challenging. It can be very difficult to analyse composite work in this way, particularly for product-model subjects where there is not a clear ordering of steps, and this is compounded by the fact that the means of nurture often do not resemble the final product, and the exercises needed for the development of student abilities may appear reductive or out of place. Nevertheless – perhaps because of this – the planning of this synthesis, from parts to wholes, is an incredibly powerful principle of sequencing, and deserves careful attention.

3.6.7 Living-in sequencing

We saw in Section 2.3 that the power of a curriculum is not located solely in the paper it is written on, and nowhere is this more true than for sequencing. While there are good sequences and bad, an excellent sequence of material can only see its qualities manifest in teaching where the sequence itself is lived-in, in Heidegger's sense, by teachers.

However good the thinking, codification, and teacher materials that go into a curriculum, if those teaching it have not spent time as a team discussing, challenging, and thinking through the progression, links, and development through a curriculum, the sequence will not work as well as it should. This is not to say that new curriculum must be built from scratch by every department, but that time for departmental work on curriculum thinking is vital. Even where materials are brought in from elsewhere, teachers need time to explore and discuss the elements of sequencing outlined here, and make appropriate adaptations, in the context of a wider engagement with the subject discourse and curricular thinking.

3.7 Conclusion to the chapter

An ability to understand the nature of curriculum, both in relation to wider knowledge and societal spheres, and internally through the manifestations of parts, strands, and approaches, will serve several purposes. Such analysis can contribute to subject-specialist curriculum thinking, allowing clarity in discussion over things such as the inclusion, development, and progression of knowledge in curriculum. It can provide a backbone for the comparative understanding required by senior leaders in order to lead well across specialisms in a school – and we shall rely on these ideas in our exploration of the subjects in the next section. And both of these strands of discourse are the foundations of the increasing professionalisation of teaching, and the movement towards schools as agents of what Oakeshott described as "the inseparability of learning and being human."[42]

3.8 Questions for discussion

3.8.1 Disciplines, subjects, and recontextualisation

- What disciplines are related to this subject?

- If your subject relates to more than one discipline, what is the nature of their combination in the subject? Is it multi-disciplinary or inter-disciplinary?

- What differences are there between your subject and its related discipline/s? What aspects from the related discipline/s is it important to stay true to in the subject?

3.8.2 Quests, gazes, truth, and approval

- What are the unique ways of looking in this subject?

- What kinds of things does this subject put into the world?

- What is it like to live-in this subject?

- What would the world be like without this subject?

- What kinds of questions does this subject ask? What answers does it give? How are those answers reached?

3.8.3 Knowledge categories

- Are substantive and disciplinary knowledge useful categories for this subject?

- What is the nature of truth in this discipline? Is it sought after? Argued about? If so, how should this be approached in curriculum?

- Is the theory/practical distinction useful in this subject? If so, what are the components and wholes in these categories? What things do we want children to learn, to be able to know and to do? What are the pieces that begin to make up these things?

- Are declarative and non-declarative or procedural knowledge useful categories for this subject? If so, where?

- What are the independently necessary pieces of knowledge for X?

- What knowledge will be cumulatively sufficient for X?

- What debates are there around the inclusion and exclusion of knowledge in curriculum for this subject?

3.8.4 Relations of knowledge

- What is the nature of the ontology of this subject? Are there many ascending conceptual levels of abstraction or explanation? Or do the areas not follow a hierarchy as such?

- How tightly defined are the relationships between areas of knowledge and between conceptual levels? Is there a tight grammar, where relations in the knowledge are deterministic and consistently agreed, and areas are strongly integrated into each other? Or are the relations more weakly determined, with a more flexible grammar and less uniform agreement about integrations?

■ What sorts of things happen when new knowledge or meaning is generated within the discipline, or when knowledge or meaning is renewed within the classroom? Are the products unified or unifying, fitting a strong integration? Or are they discursive or accumulative, bringing more to the field as a discussion or an addition, rather than a unification?

■ How does the knowledge in this subject relate cognitively for students? Are there typically specific things which must be mastered first? Or are there a number of ways of preparing for future learning, each with its own merits and none independently necessary?

■ Is the distinction of core and hinterland useful for this subject? If so, what are the relations between them? In what ways does hinterland feed the core – what would be lost if hinterland was stripped away? How do these relations look both at a point and over time?

3.8.5 Progression

■ What does it mean to get better at this subject?

■ What are the things a child should know and be able to do at the end of their time studying this curriculum? How should they be able to see the world?

■ What are the components of this knowledge that can be taught?

■ What are the exercises that can develop these abilities?

■ What can we learn from classical programmes of study (e.g. the music grade system, classical art education, etc.)

3.8.6 Knowledge over time: sequencing

■ What are the aims of the curriculum? What changes do we seek to effect in our students as a result of them studying it? What are the things that need to happen in order for those changes to be realised? What is the best order for these things?

■ How might knowledge be grouped in curriculum? Do substantive topic spines with disciplinary satellites work? Or should those roles be reversed? Are enquiry questions or projects appropriate? Should these be used throughout or should they be supplemented with different styles of units?

■ What factors contribute to a meaningful narrative here? How is this story best told?

■ What is the proximal function of X? What is its ultimate function?

■ What manthanological considerations must be taken into account? What must be known first in order to unlock X?

■ To what extent is semantic waving a useful concept for curriculum in this subject? How might the curriculum move from concrete, to abstract, to concrete again in a transfer to a new context? Over what timescales can this waving usefully happen?

■ What links exist across parts of the curriculum? How can the curriculum develop the explicit nature of those links? What should the role of interweaving be, and what might this look like?

■ What are the components of the things that we want students to be able to do by the end? How should these components be sequenced and explicitly taught? How should the bringing-together of these components be staggered and sequenced? Where should complete synthesis of parts-to-whole come?

Notes

1 See Section 2.1
2 See, for example, Section 2.2.2
3 See Oakeshott (1959)
4 Oldfield et al. (2019) p. 9
5 Bernstein (1999)
6 Ashbee (2020); see for example the changing role of climate change in the curriculum at http://se-ed.co.uk/edu/wp-content/uploads/2013/10/A-History-of-Sustainability-in-the-Curriculum.pdf
7 See Polanyi (1958)
8 See e.g. Heidegger (1927) p. 143
9 Maton (2014) pp. 94-95
10 See, for example, Hume (1739) and Descartes (1641)
11 Notwithstanding the complications around this idea.
12 Bennett (2004)
13 Ryle (1945)
14 Cohen and Squire (1980)
15 Didau (2018, 2021)
16 Fordham (2017)
17 Bernstein (1999)
18 Maton (2014)
19 Maton (2014)
20 Maton (2014)
21 See Willingham (2009) p. 134
22 Heath and Heath (2006)
23 See Section 3.5.2
24 Or at least we can say that they are as Descartes will allow us.
25 Korzybski (1995)
26 See Kuhn (1970)
27 Meyer and Land's (2003) "threshold concepts" are clearly related to manthanology, though they are probably best understood as a special case, since there are a great many conditions such as "integrative" and "irreversible" that would not be met by much knowledge still needing consideration in a manthanological vein.

28 Counsell (2018b)
29 Fordham (2020)
30 Christodoulou (2016) p. 63
31 Counsell (2017)
32 See, for example, Needham (2019), Boulton (2017), Stanford (2019)
33 Bennett (2004)
34 Counsell (2011)
35 Willingham (2004)
36 Counsell (2018a)
37 Willingham (2002)
38 See Percival (2019): prototype theory is of interest here, and the links are worth exploring further.
39 Counsell (2020) p. 101
40 Not to be confused with inter*leaving*, a technique for revision of learned material, rather than a principle of meaningful curriculum design.
41 Foster (2020)
42 Oakeshott (1989) p. 6

References

Ashbee, R. "Why It's So Important to Understand School Subjects – And How We Might Begin To Do So", in Sealy, C. (Ed.), *The researchED Guide to the Curriculum*. Woodbridge: John Catt, 2020

Bennett, A. *The History Boys*. London: Faber and Faber, 2004

Bernstein, B. "The Social Construction of Pedagogic Discourse", *Class, Codes and Control*. London: Routledge, 1999

Boulton, K. "My best planning: Part 1" on ...To The Real, 2017; available at http://...tothe-real.wordpress.com/my-best-planning-part-1/ (accessed 8.08.2019)

Christodoulou, D. *Making Good Progress?* Oxford: Oxford University Press, 2016

Cohen N. and Squire L. "Preserved Learning and Retention of Pattern Analyzing Skill in Amnesia: Dissociation of Knowing How and Knowing That" in *Science*, 210, 1980

Counsell, C. "Disciplinary Knowledge For All, The Secondary History Curriculum and History Teachers' Achievement" in *The Curriculum Journal*, 22 (2), 201–225, 2011

Counsell, C. "Review of Making Good Progress: The Future of Assessment for Learning, by Daisy Christodoulou" in *Schoolsweek*, February 16, 2017 (accessed 4.01.2020)

Counsell, C. "Senior Curriculum Leadership 1: The Indirect Manifestation of Knowledge: (A) Curriculum as Narrative", *The Dignity of the Thing*, 2018a, available at https://thedignityofthethingblog.wordpress.com/2018/04/07/senior-curriculum-leadership-1-the-indirect-manifestation-of-knowledge-a-curriculum-as-narrative/ (accessed 4.01.2020)

Counsell, C. "Senior Curriculum Leadership 1: The Indirect Manifestation of Knowledge: (B) Final Performance as Deceiver and Guide", *The Dignity of the Thing*, 2018b, available at https://thedignityofthethingblog.wordpress.com/ (accessed 13.02.20)

Counsell, C. "Taking Curriculum Seriously" in *Impact – Journal of the Chartered College of Teaching*, 4: 2018c, available at: https://impact.chartered.college/article/taking-curriculum-seriously/ (accessed 13.02.2020)

Counsell, C. "Better Conversations with Subject Leaders" in Sealy, C. (Ed.) *The researchED Guide to the Curriculum*. Woodbridg: John Catt, 2020

Descartes, R. *Meditations*. London: Penguin, 1641/2010

Didau, D. *Making Kids Cleverer*. Carmarthen: Crown House 2018

Didau, D. *Making Meaning in English*. London: Routledge, 2021

Fordham, M. "Knowledge: Independently Necessary or Collectively Sufficient?", *Clio et cetera*, 2017, available at https://clioetcetera.com/2017/01/05/knowledge-independent-ly-necessary-or-collectively-sufficient/ (accessed 3.02.2020)

Fordham, M. "What did I mean by 'the curriculum is the progression model?" *Clio et cetera*, 2020, available at https://clioetcetera.com/2020/02/08/what-did-i-mean-by-the-curricu-lum-is-the-progression-model/ (accessed 3.03.2020)

Foster, R. "On Weaving an English Curriculum", *The Learning Profession*, 2020, availa-ble at https://thelearningprofession.com/2020/07/30/weaving-an-english-curriculum/ (accessed 1.08.2020)

Heath, C. and Heath, D. "The Curse of Knowledge" in *Harvard Busines Review*, December 2006, available at: https://hbr.org/2006/12/the-curse-of-knowledge (accessed 13.02.2020)

Heidegger, M. *Being and Time*. (Trans. Stambaugh, J.) Albany: State University of New York Press, 1927/1953

Hume, D. *A Treatise of Human Nature*. Oxford: Oxford University Press, 1739/2008

Korzybski, A. *Science and Sanity: An Introduction to Non-Aristotelian Systems and General Semantics*. New York: Institute of General Semantics, 1995

Kuhn, T. *The Structure of Scientific Revolutions*. Chicago: University of Chicago Press, 1970

Maton, K. *Knowledge and Knowers*. Abingdon: Routledge, 2014

Meyer, J.H.F. and Land, R. "Threshold Concepts and Troublesome Knowledge: Linkages to Ways of Thinking and Practising", in Rust, C. (Ed.), *Improving Student Learning - Theory and Practice Ten Years On*, pp. 412–424. Oxford: Oxford Centre for Staff and Learning Development (OCSLD), 2003

Needham, T. "Analytical Introductions", *Tom Needham Teach*, Jan 2019, available at https://tomneedhamteach.wordpress.com/analytical-introductions (accessed 20.12.2019)

Oakeshott, M. *The Voice of Poetry in the Conversation of Mankind: An Essay*. London: Bowes and Bowes, 1959

Oakeshott, M. "A Place of Learning" in *The Voice of Liberal Learning*. Indiana: Liberty Fund, 1989

Oldfield, S., et al. Norfolk Agreed Syllabus 2019, 2019, available at https://www.schools.nor-folk.gov.uk/-/media/schools/files/teaching-and-learning/religious-education-agreed-syl-labus/norfolk-religious-education-agreed-syllabus-2019.pdf (accessed 15.05.2020)

Percival, A. "Three Ways to Tackle Common Pupil Misconceptions", *Times Educational Supplement*, 2019, available at https://www.tes.com/news/3-ways-tackle-common-pu-pil-misconceptions (accessed 11.8.2020)

Polanyi, M. *Personal Knowledge: Towards a Post-Critical Philosophy*. London: Routledge, 1958

Ryle, G. "Knowing How and Knowing That", in *Proceedings of the Aristotelian Society*, 46, 1945

Stanford, M. "Did the Bretons break?" in *Teaching History*, 175, 8–14, 2019

Willingham, D. 2002. "Ask the Cognitive Scientist: Inflexible Knowledge: The First Step to Expertise", *Researchgate*, available at https://www.researchgate.net/profile/Daniel_Willingham/publication/234665275_Ask_the_Cognitive_Scientist_Inflexible_Knowledge_The_First_Step_to_Expertise/ (accessed 21.8.2020)

Willingham, D. "The Privileged Status of Story", *American Educator*, 2004, available at https://www.aft.org/periodical/american-educator/summer-2004/ask-cognitive-scientist (accessed 4.02.20)

Willingham, D. *Why Don't Students Like School?* San Francisco: Jossey-Bass, 2009

4 THE SUBJECTS

An introduction to the subjects

We turn now to the subject specialisms. Each of these sections seeks to portray the essence of the subject, an explication of its quests, gazes, and the nature and structure of its knowledge. These analyses draw on the curriculum theories laid out in Chapter 3, study of the subjects themselves, and reflections from the specialist discourse. Central to each subject section is a figure laying out some suggested key strands of knowledge and their relationships within the subject. Through these short subject sections, it is hoped, non-specialists can gain a window onto the specialisms that can open up the discourse across the divide. The gap between specialist and non-specialist can never be filled, but it can be bridged, and that is our aim here.

Senior curriculum leaders should have an appreciation for all of the subjects. They must be able to glimpse the existential wonder and joy of the specialist, to have a sense of what it means to live-in each of the subjects, with all its knowledge and ways-of-looking. As educated people we are all members of the "great conversations of humankind" and we should be explicitly aware of both the existence of these great conversations, and how great they truly are, in order to authentically lead, and indeed champion, the subject specialisms in schools.

As we have said, the discourse is, and should be, diverse and in flux. The analyses offered here are just that, offerings. I hope and expect others will add to and challenge these submissions; it is in such exchanges that thinking flourishes. Many specialists have characterised their subjects far more eloquently than either space or specialism permit here; it is hoped that in drawing such work together in synoptic if brief summaries, and in suggesting questions for discussion and further specialist reading, that the quality of understanding and discussions in schools in relation to curriculum and the subject specialisms can be strengthened.

The ideas laid out here offer starting points for understanding, to begin to build protection against harmful genericist approaches, to structure discussion with subject leaders, and to point towards avenues to develop the curriculum thinking and participation within departments. All of these things must be at the core of strong curriculum work in a school.

A great deal that should be made explicit in our efforts to induct students into ongoing curricular conversations often remains implicit or tacitly assumed, with the result that important material is not planned for or taught well enough to deliver a truly ambitious and powerful curriculum. Because subject specialists are so immersed in their subjects, identifying the components of what should be taught can be very challenging. Conversations around the analyses presented here should therefore be of use to both specialists working on curriculum as well as senior curriculum leaders. The aim is always to make the hidden and assumed, visible and considered, so that its explicit teaching in curriculum may be planned. Ultimately, of course, these conversations must extend far beyond the headlines given here, deep into the specialist discourse, where the detail of substance can begin to be explored in fullness.

The purpose of the analysis in these sections, then, is to support clear thinking and discussion. But lurking in the shadows of analysis is the spectre of reductionism. In studying components, and giving names to things, we must guard against the tendency to turn names into disaggregated units, and useful distinctions into impenetrable barriers. The knowledge in subjects is inescapably organic, overlapping, and interconnected, just as the human body is. Analysing knowledge into parts and their relationships is illuminating, just as studying organs and systems is for students of medicine. But doctors and curriculum thinkers alike must understand the whole beyond the analysis of parts, in order for patients and subjects to flourish.

Sequencing matters, as we have seen. It is common, when discussing the subjects, to proceed in something like the following order: English, Mathematics, Science, History, Geography and so on, down some perceived hierarchy or list of importance or core-ness. However, such a sequence carries little meaning in terms of knowledge. Here, we follow a path through the subjects according to their quests. We travel first through the descriptive quests, merging over into the interpretive, before turning to the expressive, and finally the solving-producing, with the understanding that, of course, many subjects in reality encompass more than one of these quest-types.

It should go without saying that these characterisations and groupings are themselves open to debate and such debates can no doubt spark illuminating discussion. There are undoubtedly other groupings and sequences that can be meaningful, as is so often the case with any group of ideas. Although different – and useful – meanings could no doubt be made with different sequences, it is hoped that meaning can be made from *this* route, and with our path now laid out with all its caveats, let us turn to the first subject on our journey.

Mathematics

The existence of things like numbers and shapes, their occupation of an abstract plane completely independent of the tangible and concrete, and the entirely consistent and predictable way these concepts behave, have been a source of fascination to some of humanity's finest minds since the earliest civilisations. We find ourselves in a universe where the physical realm behaves in mathematical ways, and where mathematics can be applied to yield many descriptive, predictive, and material gains. The book of nature, as Galileo said, is written in the language of mathematics.

Without exception, the objects of mathematics behave according to rules. This is significant, and accounts for both the nature of the claims made by mathematics, and the practices of its knowledge production. The quest of mathematics is to uncover and describe these rules governing the inhabitants of the abstract plane, to find the laws of these realms and explore their implications and applications. Because this sphere is so unlike the concrete, physical, everyday world, a large body of mathematics is devoted to the notations, conventions and procedures that can allow calculations to be carried out. New knowledge is made in mathematics in the postulations, developments, and proofs of conjectures, and in developing new techniques and applications, in both pure and applied mathematics.

Because of the near-perfect internal consistency and logic of mathematics, the role of the subjective in the discipline is in some ways slim. Most mathematics can be proven incontrovertibly within its own axioms. This is not to say, though, that the individual or knower does not matter. Mathematical discoveries are made by people, with intent, and they are made when people make leaps, when they make new meaning from what was already there. The aforementioned axioms are a matter for the subjective too: by definition, axioms must be chosen and accepted without reference to any higher principles; and axioms are indeed the subject of significant argument amongst mathematicians.

Students of mathematics are brought into a unique way of seeing and behaving: to reach out into the intangible sphere of mathematical objects and their relations, and to know that problems can be solved and discoveries made – through mathematical processes, through the manipulation of rational bodies, through the specialist notation that makes it possible. To see the behaviour of mathematics and to live-in it is to see rational, elegant truth in the world, and it is beautiful.

School mathematics is highly recontextualised in that the curriculum looks very different to the work carried out by mathematicians today; due to the strong independent necessity of the manthanology within mathematics, the objects of the curriculum at school level are several orders removed from those of people working on mathematical knowledge in the field of production. The approaches and methods of working, the following of procedures, elimination of possibilities, and the concept of proof are however lived in the practice of both school and practising mathematics; the recontextualised difference is in the precise objects of that gaze.

The school mathematics curriculum is typically categorised according to the following areas: number, algebra, shape, ratio and proportion, probability, and statistics, and in some places a separate area called "mathematical reasoning" or equivalent. Figure 4.1 shows a representation of the relationships between these areas.[1]

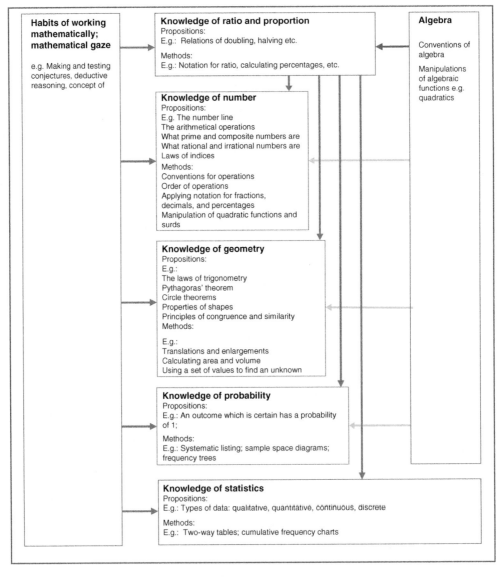

Figure 4.1 Knowledge in mathematics curriculum

At the core of the knowledge in school mathematics we can conceptualise the four areas of number, geometry, probability, and statistics. Within each of these we can identify declarative and procedural knowledge, or propositions and methods respectively. Let us look at these areas in turn.

1. Number is the area of mathematics dealing with the properties and behaviours of numbers. Over history, the discipline of mathematics has developed notations and conventions for representing and handling numbers, their relationships and interactions. Thus the arithmetical operations, the rules for handling fractions, decimals and indices, and the procedures for manipulation of functions can all be understood as examples of knowledge in the area of number (though they are by no means confined to it).

2. Geometry is the study of shape and space. Points, lines, two-dimensional and three-dimensional shapes all follow a specific, internally consistent set of rules. In addition to the cataloguing of these rules and the use of them to find unknowns, geometry has its own set of conventions, notations, and procedures for solving geometrical problems, such as translations and enlargements.

3. Probability is the branch of mathematics concerned with chance. Outcomes of events, and samples from groups, can often not be determined but they can be treated mathematically. Statistics concerns the handling and processing of data from the world in order to draw conclusions and make meaning from that data.

4. Statistics covers the processing and analysis of large sets of data, taken from the concrete world, the drawing of inferences and conclusions from those data, and the evaluation of uncertainty about those conclusions.

Because of the abstract nature of mathematics, it has its own notation and language. The conventions and terminology that form part of that language are curricular objects in their own right, and warrant explicit consideration and standardisation across the curriculum, within and across the areas described.

Knowledge in mathematics is incredibly densely linked, in that any of these core areas could be linked in a mathematical problem or question. However, there are two areas of knowledge that consistently overarch each of the core four. The concepts of ratio and proportion apply to number, geometry, probability, and statistics, since variables or quantities in these areas can always be compared mathematically. And algebra, while often seen as an area of knowledge on a similar basis to the core four in this map, is perhaps better understood as a language and set of notations that allows us to explore the relationships in each of the core four, as well as in ratio and proportion.

All of these areas can be understood as representing the substantive knowledge of mathematics: the meaning and claims that the subject puts into the world, and the associated procedures for that meaning. What then, of the disciplinary dimension? Suffusing over all of these areas is the gaze of the mathematics student and the habits of participating in mathematics, and the general principles of mathematical investigation and problem solving. These approaches and ways of working can be seen to represent the disciplinary dimension of school mathematics.

The ontology of mathematics, then, is composed both of claims about the world and of methods. The architecture of this ontology can be understood as very tall, with many conceptual layers of abstraction and composition along both claims and methods. For example, circle theorems can be proved using Euclid's five axioms of geometry; solving linear equations is a composite of arithmetic operations, order of operations, substitution, and simplifying. The grammar or integration of knowledge in mathematics is very strong with relations being highly integrated, with very little dispute over the nature of these relations (except in some areas at the very boundaries of mathematics and philosophy in the field of production).

Epistemologically, knowledge in mathematics typically proceeds by solving problems incontrovertibly, adding knowledge in unification to the tightly bound architecture described. In the field of production, a proof might be put forward that can be shown to be consistent, allowing a new claim to be put forward about the world of numbers or geometry. Other areas of development are in the creation of new methods, such as Newton's and Leibniz's calculus or the various developments of Bayesian statistics. Elsewhere, novel applications of techniques push forward the boundaries of applied mathematics, such as in cryptography or modelling of vortices. In the classroom, participation in mathematics typically prepares for these epistemological patterns: in the practice of mathematical techniques, gaining familiarity with the claims of mathematics, and developing ability to solve problems and test conjectures.

Manthanologically, we find an almost entirely independent necessity of prior knowledge in mathematics. It is not possible, for example, to learn to solve linear equations (at least in any robust sense) without having first mastered the arithmetic operations, order of operations, substitution and simplifying previously stated as the components of this area. Thus the sequencing, assessment for learning, and responsive teaching[2] of mathematics are highly contingent on this manthanology.

These very distinctive characteristics of mathematics can inform thinking in many areas of mathematics curriculum work, and can offer light in the delineation of the subject as a specialism that is really very different, in many ways, to all others.

Questions for discussion

- What are the facts and methods that should make up the curriculum? What are the links between these?

- What is the necessary prior knowledge needed in order to access X? What are the component steps or fundamental explanations?

- What are the conventions of mathematics that students must be taught? What are the ways of looking? What features of the curriculum induct students into a mathematician's way of approaching the world?

- What synoptic work is planned to explicitly draw links across the areas?

- What are the questions/problems that students will be able to solve? What is the level of difficulty of these? What is it that makes them challenging? What are the components of these questions and where are they taught?

- Which methods are taught to students and why?

Science

In science we look for patterns in things; to explain why things are as they are; to see the future in predictions. The natural world – the world of matter, forces, energy, cells, and organisms – seems to follow a tight structure of causality, making it amenable to the scientific method of study and the revealing of beautiful regularities and elegant explanations.

The empiricist gaze is fundamental to the scientific outlook. In science, we don't just look for patterns or explanations, and then look away if none are found. We design experiments, isolate variables, find novel ways in which to lay bare what was once hidden. There is, in science, an intentional and dialectic interaction with the physical world, and a quest for truth and reflection of reality.

This is not to say that science is a direct channel to objective truth. Mathematical and determinist objects, such as we find in science, allow mathematical and determinist *study*, but the conclusions reached are always *gestalts*, leaps: they always are integrative of *more than just the data*, since they go beyond the data. Though we have never seen an electron, for example, we have detailed theories about their behaviour, and those theories explain things from chemical reactions, to circuits, to colours. The role of the scientist – the subject and the subjective – in reaching these conclusions and in living-in them as a practitioner is a significant though often overlooked aspect of the discipline of science.[3]

Science's quest, then, is to describe and explain the natural world, to uncover the hidden pieces, principles, and processes that make up the world and that make things happen in it. Science seeks to explain why things are as they are, to find, name and relate the things that make up other things, and to discover the patterns that lie beneath. In living-in science, students experience the universe as a fundamentally governed object, subject to rules and principles, beautiful and awe-inspiring architecture behind the everyday: Newton's laws, atomic theory, natural selection, and so on. Students experience the lens of empiricism, and the idea that certain claims have a referent in reality, and can be tested, and found to be false, and that this is a defence against charlatanism and deceit. The satisfaction in being able to explain so many things – and in knowing that there is an explanation, even if it is currently not known, for so many more – is a joy and a wonder. This is the essence of science.

Figure 4.2 shows us how we might conceive of knowledge in science.[4]

In what we might understand as the substantive knowledge of science, we put forward a set of claims about the world: descriptions of the physical, chemical, and biological objects in the world, stars, molecules, ecosystems, and all the things in between. We also describe the laws that govern those things: theories of energy, bonding, interdependence, and so on. We detail the processes these things undergo, and the links between all of these objects, laws, principles, and

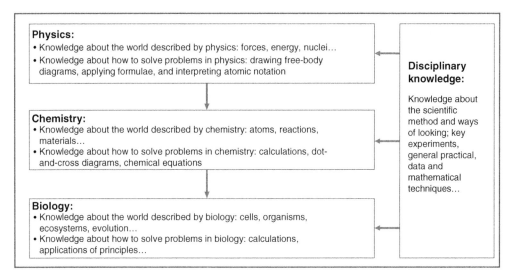

Figure 4.2 Knowledge in science curriculum

processes. In science we describe, explain, and predict. We say what things are made of and why they behave as they do. We seek to find quantitative relationships between things wherever possible. Many of these statements of meaning about the world are accompanied by specialist techniques and procedures for renewing meaning, from drawing free-body and dot-and-cross diagrams to applying formulae to predict values for quantities. Much of this knowledge in science is abstract, unfamiliar, and counter-intuitive, and the fascination of the true but surprising, from mechanics to combustion, is one of the delights well-known to the disciple of science.

New knowledge in science is made by discoveries, adding new phenomena to existing frameworks, confirming predictions or sometimes tearing up earlier theories and replacing with new ones. This unificatory epistemology reflects, or at least it is scientists' hope that it does, an ontological architecture of layers of cause and manifestation, and single objective truth. Science's ontology is therefore very tall: there are key fundamental principles such as the conservation of energy that underlie and integrate a great many other areas. This knowledge is very densely linked: photosynthesis, for example, is related to atoms, energy, adaptation, cells, respiration and many more things besides. The nature of these links is complex: explanatory, part-whole, or causal, but they are consistently strongly integrated, and they are critical to the gaze of science, in which unification is cherished, and a route back from any phenomenon to universal laws is prized.

Alongside all of the substantive claims and specialist procedures of the knowledge in science sits knowledge of scientific methods, or what we might call the disciplinary strand of science. While the application and even existence of a true or consistent scientific method is contested by philosophers of science, its status even as an ideal is core to the gaze of science and its recontextualised curriculum.

The processes of hypothesis, experimental design, practical experimentation, and data analysis and interpretation, and the wider setting of this process in terms of peer-review and publication, are key to understanding both how science seeks to proceed and the status of the claims made by scientists. Scientific conclusions, of course, are always underdetermined, and can never be known for certain to be true, but they can certainly be indicated to be false. Understanding this is an important element in both an appreciation of the claims of science, and participation in democratic society.

Linked to both the substantive and disciplinary knowledge in science is knowledge of mathematics, which pertains to both the substantive laws of physics and chemistry, and to handling the data of the empiricist. Thus mathematics is deeply related to the truth-claims of science and is a significant feature in strong science curriculum.

Knowledge in the substantive strand in science has a significant necessity to its manthanology: many things in science will not make sense unless knowledge of particular requisite concepts has already been acquired. As a result, there is broad agreement over some elements of curriculum structure and sequencing. Much rich debate in the discourse, however, centres around contested areas of sequencing, and how best meaning might be made from the order of teaching.

Questions for discussion

■ What are the pieces of knowledge that should be included in the curriculum? What are the links between them?

■ What are the scientific ways of looking at the world into which students should be inducted? How should the curriculum build this induction?

■ What are the requisite pieces of prior knowledge for X? Where are they taught?

■ What are the links between X and other parts of the curriculum? How should students be taught to see these links?

■ What are the components of working scientifically/disciplinary knowledge and how should they be mapped for progression?

■ How does knowledge of key substantive concepts develop throughout the curriculum?

■ How does the curriculum help students to see the boundary conditions of science: the sorts of claims it can and cannot make, and the sorts of questions it can and cannot ask/answer?

■ What should be the role of practical work in science curriculum?

Geography

Understanding the Earth, its atmosphere, the activities of humans on its surface, and the interactions between all of these things is the quest of geography. Geography has a fundamentally interdisciplinary nature and brings together elements of geology, meteorology, biology, economics, politics, and many other specialisms. The objects of the study of geography, and the sorts of questions geography seeks to answer, require it to draw on such multiple disciplines in synopsis and synthesis. Thus, while geography seeks descriptions and explanations of things in the world, it differs from science in its methods and in the nature of knowledge it produces. It would not make sense for geography to have the highly integrated and tall ontology of science, as it necessarily makes use of knowledge from diverse fields, with equally diverse structures.

We find a corresponding heterogeneity in the statuses of truth and the natures of meaning within geography. There are relatively straightforward observational claims, such as the compositions of various soils; there is modelling and extrapolation of complex, multi-variable data leading to contested conclusions, such as theory of plate tectonics; and we find lenses and ideology in interpretations, especially in questions of human geography such as world development.[5] Through this rich diversity of objects, relations with the world, and construction of claims, geographical meaning is made.

Through geography, children experience a connection between world, place, and interactions. They are able to place events on the global landscape, to give a background to geopolitical events, to access discussions of politics, economics, environment, and place. In geography, we can see, question, and explore the interactions and tensions between human existence and the surface of our planet.[6] Through this knowledge comes awareness and access that all children should be entitled to, both because these things are intrinsically valuable, and because they are crucial to informed participation in democratic society.

Substantive knowledge in geography is typically analysed according to two frameworks: physical and human geography (with the intersection being environmental geography) and locational and place knowledge, these being the knowledge of where things are in the world and the knowledge of the features of places respectively. The disciplinary knowledge in geography – of taking samples, interpreting data, and forming reports and synoptic answers to questions – can be understood as sitting alongside these groups, with particular relevance for each. Figure 4.3 gives us a way of conceiving of these strands of knowledge.[7,8]

Crucial to this map are the interactions of the areas with one another. Geography is not just concerned with the features of the Earth and the activities of humans: it is also the interplay and dialectic, and causal, relationships of these things that are objects of exploration and thought in geographical work.[9]

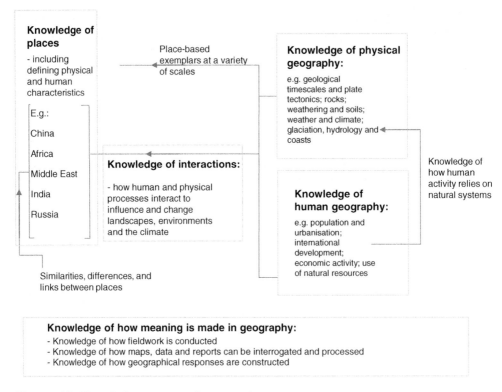

Figure 4.3 Knowledge in geography curriculum

The substantive knowledge in geography is much flatter in its ontology and weaker in its integration than science and mathematics. The intrinsically interdisciplinary nature of geography means that while there are many concepts, explanations, and fundamentals, they do not unite in the highly grammatical way we find in more uniform subjects. In geography there are a great many concepts, such as pressure, absolute and relative poverty, and sustainability, but they occupy diverse areas of knowledge, with contested links, and do not structure the knowledge in a tightly organised way as is found in science and mathematics. Geography has an overall moderate semantic gravity: contexts and details are important in a way we don't find in science and mathematics. The relations between abstract or fundamental principles and ideas on one hand, and specific contexts and cases, with all their details, on the other, are ends-in-themselves for this subject. The goal in geography is not just to understand the principles – it is to understand complex and concrete cases in themselves as well: principles help us to reach this understanding, but they are not in themselves enough.[10] The role of hinterland knowledge – of details that build understanding of the richness of the concrete in geography – is significant, and breadth and specifics of examples and cases explored must be understood as essential to the nature of the subject.

Epistemologically, knowledge in geography is in places unificatory, in others accumulative, and in still others discursive. In some areas, theories are corroborated or rejected because of evidence, as in the case of plate tectonics and the slab-pull theory; in other areas, geographical work is put forward and accumulated into the discourse, without being a direct integration or manifestation of some other work, and without increasing any ontological layers in the discipline – for example, a discussion of agriculture in Less Economically Developed Countries (LEDCs). In this way, the width of the ontology is increased, since there are more examples and details contributing to the body of knowledge. In other areas, alternative interpretations are contributed as part of an ongoing discussion, as with the various models for understanding urban development, such as the competing Burgess and Hoyt models. As a result of this often widening but not heightening ontology, a significant amount, though not all, of geographical scholarship from the field of production is both accessible and relevant to the school curriculum.

Another difference we find in geography is the more prominent role of the knower and the subjective. Because of the often compositional and judgment-forming nature of geographical work, and the production of written pieces as geographical responses rather than just right-or-wrong solutions, the personal schema of the knower necessarily has a bearing on geographical work, particularly in human geography. Lenses and interpretations have a more overt disciplinary significance in a way not found in maths and science. Thus, in the field of production at least, we find positivist geography, critical geography, and so on. While it is rare for these approaches to be explicitly taught in the secondary school curriculum, it is worth considering that lenses of one sort or another will be present, whether or not they are made explicit, in those working on the geography curriculum. These lenses will also be developed to a greater or lesser extent in the students of that curriculum, as an intrinsic feature of the nature of the subject.

Links between knowledge in geography are both extensive and crucial. Every location on Earth has its characteristics determined by the effect and interplay of the numerous physical and human geographical factors present: the natural resources, the climate, the population, infrastructure, economic development, and so on. Each of these factors can influence or be influenced by others, either directly or indirectly. Places are linked to other places, through proximity, trade, tourism, and migration. Additionally, places can be compared by studying the similarities and differences in the inputs and outcomes of any of these factors, creating conceptual links even where physical ones are absent. If you want to relate one item of geographical knowledge to another you probably can, and will find out something interesting by doing so. This high semantic density is a key feature of knowledge relations in geography.

Sitting alongside these substantive areas is the disciplinary knowledge of geography: knowledge of how research is conducted, sources interpreted, and data presented. The craft of the geographer, in producing responses, in particular in writing geographical work, can be understood as a curricular object in itself, worthy of explicit analysis and mapping across the curriculum along with all the other knowledge in geography.[11]

Progression in geography then, can be understood as following all of these strands: knowing more physical and human geography, knowing more about the links between areas of geography, knowing more about how research is conducted, and becoming more able to interpret sources and construct geographical responses. The components of these areas, and their mapping, are key to geography curriculum. Knowledge in geography can be understood as having a mixture of cumulative and necessary manthanology, with some components or foundations critically necessary for the accessing of certain curriculum areas, while for others a number of alternative routes have equal merit. Many concepts can contribute to analysis of case studies, but it would often not be wise to teach all concepts before studying any examples, for example. In sequencing geography curriculum, thought must be given not just to the strands and components of knowledge, but to the significance of developing connections across them and of building a rich hinterland that students can bring to a highly synoptic subject. In this vein, the use of enquiry questions as a structuring device in geography curriculum has been a productive area of the subject discourse for some years.[12]

Questions for discussion

- How should the curriculum help students develop a sense of location and place?

- What are the key human and physical geography ideas that should be taught? How should these be sequenced?

- What case studies and examples should be used to develop understanding of key geographical ideas?

- What are the important details of these case studies and examples?

- How can students be taught to apply knowledge of geographical ideas and concepts to new examples?

- What are the key geographical skills that should be taught? What are the components of these skills? What exercises relate to these components?

- What are the features of excellent writing in geography? How should these be mapped and explicitly taught across the curriculum?

- What does excellent scholarship look like in geography? Who are the best writers?

- What role can geographical scholarship play in the curriculum?

- What might the role of enquiry questions be in the curriculum?

History

History, in seeking to understand the past, has a descriptivist and explanationist quest. However, this is not straightforward. We have seen how even science, the archetypally objectivist discipline, relies on the subjective to make meaning from data, to construct theories that reach beyond the empirical. We saw how geography, with its swirling of many variables, disciplines, and often human objects of study, in individuals, communities, ideas, and institutions, brings in a more prominent role for the knower and their interpretation, although this is rarely made explicit in school curricula. In history, meaning is made almost exclusively about human subjects and attached ideas: the shifting of power, the features of societies, the development of institutions, and so on. All of these things are intangible, underdetermined, and emergent from the behaviour of groups of individuals and their interactions with the world. As such the creation of meaning in the subject relies heavily on the interpretation of the knower, whilst simultaneously being informed by evidence. That evidence is always, and necessarily, incomplete: we must draw on the sources that have survived, and of course not on those that have been lost or destroyed; those sources are often in themselves already necessarily partially subjectified in that they are products of people. Therefore history is at once descriptive, explanatory, and interpretive.

The production of knowledge in history follows several "agreed historical procedures – careful, systematic readings of historical evidence, establishing its provenance, purpose and bias, cross-referencing different sources, and establishing what other historians have made of the evidence".[13] These procedures mean that it is not the case that in history "anything goes" – claims can be shown to be false by comparing them to historical evidence – but that

> accounts of the past are always interpretive and always open to dispute and question. The discipline of history is both less than the past (because not all of the past can be understood) and more than the past (because our accounts of the past are overlaid by our assumptions and presuppositions).[14]

In school history, students seldom (though it's possible that they could) interact with original sources, or spend time in the archives. However, the work of both interpretation of sources and the use of evidence to make meaning, and the awareness of this as a fundamental feature of history, is an explicit part of school history curricula. This has not always been the case, but has been the outcome of extensive debate and work by history teachers and the subject community.

Through history curriculum, students are brought into the great conversations of our institutions, our changing culture, ideas, and society, our relationship with those who have come before us, and our relationship with knowledge, our eternal

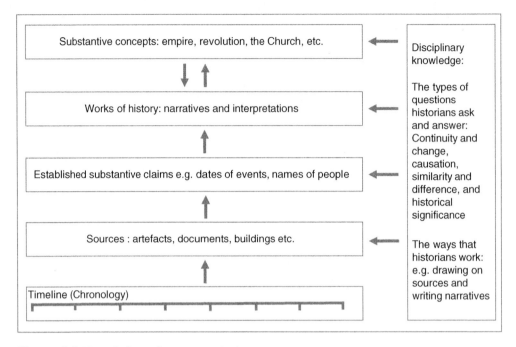

Figure 4.4 Knowledge in history curriculum

struggle and joy in the tension between subject and object, the respectful argument in which intellectuals in a discursive subject engage.

Let us turn to the knowledge in history, which could be represented using Figure 4.4.

Epistemologically, the starting point is the sources used by historians – the surviving objects and documents from the past – and the knowledge of the content of these. Then there are broadly agreed claims about the past, such as the dates of coronations, the names of people in official posts, and suchlike. These tend to be evidenced by the sources with little debate or controversy and might be called established substantive knowledge. Then we have the works of historians themselves: narratives, claims, interpretations; tapestries woven from the threads thrown out by sources; meaning made for the reader. These works of history are inevitably either explicitly or implicitly the answers to certain types of question: questions of causation and consequence, continuity and change, similarity and difference, and significance.[15] We might call the claims in these works – such as "Rex was a dirty word in Rome" or "Protestantism played a significant role in the Enlightenment" – contested or contestable substantive claims.

Emergent from and tributary to these works of history are the substantive concepts of history: revolution, empire, the Church, the peasantry, and so on. And suffusing all of this, enabling the production of all of its meaning and supporting an accurate understanding of the diverse nature of these meanings, is the disciplinary strand in history: the knowledge of how meaning is made in history; how historians operate in their use of sources and argument; how much can be agreed and what must be expected to be discursive and debated. This disciplinary knowledge is typically understood through "second order concepts" in school history curricula: significance, continuity and change, cause and consequence, similarity and difference, evidence, and interpretations.[16] The term historiography is often used here too, to denote the study of the methods of historians, the status of truth in history, and other philosophical aspects of the discipline.

There are many ways to map this knowledge. One powerful historical concept is the chronological axis, the idea that events happen over time and relate to each other over time. In a sense, all of the other substantive strands exist in relation to this timeline, and it is a significant structure in the schemata of the historian.

This knowledge has a moderately tall ontological architecture, since there are several conceptual layers of increasing abstraction or at least removal from the concrete sphere. In spite of this, abstraction does not have the same status here that it has in mathematics and science; the particulars and details of individual areas in history are always significant. The goal of history is not just to explain the concrete using the abstract, it is to understand (or rather interpret) each concrete episode in its own right. This knowledge can be understood to be fairly weakly integrated, with links being often flexible or open to contest or differing interpretations. Thus the slave trade and the Industrial Revolution, for example, can be said to be linked, but the nature of this link is not agreed within the discipline and thus manifests in the flexible grammar in the subject.

Manthanologically speaking, much of the knowledge in history can be understood as following collective sufficiency, with readiness for a certain area of study being craftable in a number of ways, with few single individually necessary components. Knowledge in history is epistemologically accumulative and discursive, and in their participation in the discipline, students will produce their own contributions to this discourse.

The components of progression in history can be analysed along several axes. To learn well in history is to learn both established and contested substantive claims in development of both core and hinterland knowledge. It is to develop understanding of substantive concepts, both as abstract ideas but crucially as well in their instances and specifics. It is to gain sophistication in the disciplinary understandings of historians, of the ways of treating and responding to historical questions, and the ways of looking at the world as historians do.[17] It is to become better at the writing of historical responses, a curricular object which, although highly contingent on context-specific knowledge, has elements which can be developed and transferred over time, with characteristic features of historical writing that can be explicitly taught, practised, and refined.

The mutually dependent relationship between the substantive and disciplinary strands are at the heart of history curriculum progression, and the reciprocity of writing and understanding is marked.[18] The two-way relationship between the substantive and disciplinary is often navigated through the use of enquiry questions,[19] and questions of recontextualisation. How far students can be taken in interacting with genuine and challenging historical and historiographical issues is a fascinating feature of the subject discourse. Areas such as narrative and cumulative sufficiency of substantive knowledge in history, and the components and synthesis of the disciplinary, are key to the discourse, and have been extensively explored in the work of several key thinkers in the subject community.[20]

Because of the accumulative and discursive epistemological nature of knowledge in history, the work of historians is often a powerful addition to the history curriculum, and can furnish many things. Excerpts from works of history can provide a way of leading students through an event to cover substantive claims; they can be an opportunity to explore interpretations; they can be analysed and emulated to develop students' writing (and thinking). In these ways, students can be brought to understanding not only important events and episodes of the past, but also the historian's way of looking, the complex relation of the knower with the world, and the fascination that is held in weaving meaning, in reading and writing history, with what is left from the past.

Questions for discussion

■ What knowledge is cumulatively sufficient in order for students to access X?

■ What are the periods, enquiry questions, substantive details and substantive concepts that should be included?

■ How should core and hinterland knowledge be developed throughout the curriculum?

■ What are the components of disciplinary knowledge and how should they be developed through the curriculum?

■ What does it mean to get better at writing about causation/significance/similarity and difference/continuity and change? What examples of scholarship can students study in order to demonstrate this? What vocabulary is needed for this type of writing? What types of sentences, and what kinds of structuring of argument? How will all of these be mapped across the curriculum, taught explicitly, and practised?

■ How does the history curriculum deal with the contested nature of the knowledge in the discipline? What substantive knowledge is treated as established and what is discussed as interpretation, and why?

■ Is the history curriculum free from ahistorical ideas and anachronism? Is the work in the history curriculum true to the discipline? Does it encourage students to develop the gaze of the historian, to see the world as historians do?

Religious studies

Religion represents perhaps humanity's oldest search for meaning beyond ourselves: a search for the reason of things; for the best ways of living; for knowledge of the divine. The role of religion in history, in the development of culture, the arts, philosophy, even of science, has been pivotal at almost every stage in their stories, and this influence is manifest in myriad ways in present-day institutions, customs, language and beliefs. Our social, political, and economic discourses are permeated by the effects of religion both throughout history and in the present day.

The list of "great conversations" into which students are inducted through a religious studies curriculum is therefore long. Any understanding of history, literature, music, and art will of course be richly furnished by an understanding of religions that have influenced those spheres, as will discussions of many contemporary social and political issues. Religions and the associated discourses are intrinsically fascinating and worthy of study in their own right, as bodies of thought, literature, and customs.

There is significant debate over the nature of religious studies. While it is broadly agreed that it is an interdisciplinary subject, the particulars of those disciplines are contested. The widely cited Norfolk Agreed Syllabus[21] suggests theology (in a broad, cross-religion sense), philosophy, and social sciences as the disciplinary strands of religious studies, while it has been argued elsewhere that history[22] and history of art[23] should also be included. There is also ongoing discussion over the inclusion of "worldviews" and the incorporation of, for example, humanism in the religious studies curriculum.

The ways of looking in religious studies – the theologian's exploration within a religious paradigm, the philosopher's working through from principles to conclusions, the social scientist's use of observation and empirical data for complex, human situations, the historian's sense of narrative and interpretation, and the art historian's hermeneutic gaze at the many key expressions of religious belief and exaltation throughout the history of art – all of these can be keys to valuable discourse both in the fields themselves and beyond.

Let us consider here just the three strands suggested in the Norfolk Agreement:

Theology enables pupils to grapple with questions that have been raised by religions and worldviews over the centuries. It looks at where beliefs come from, how they have changed over time, how they are applied differently in different contexts and how they relate to each other. It involves investigating key texts and traditions within different religions and worldviews. It explores the ways in which they have been used as authoritative for believers and the ways in which they have been challenged, interpreted and disregarded over time. It assesses the key beliefs of religions and worldviews as well as exploring the significance of experience on the claims made by religious and nonreligious people.[24]

Philosophy enables pupils to grapple with questions that have been raised and answers about knowledge, existence and morality. It is about finding out how and whether things make sense. It deals with questions of morality and ethics. It takes seriously questions about reality, knowledge and existence. The process of reasoning lies at the heart of philosophy. Philosophy is less about coming up with answers to difficult questions and more about the process of how we try to answer them. Studying the works of great philosophers is part of developing an understanding of philosophy. It uses dialogue, discussion and debate to refine the way in which we think about the world and our place in it. Philosophy contains three fields of enquiry which are applicable to a balanced framework for RE. These are metaphysics, logic and moral philosophy.[25]

The human/social sciences enable pupils to grapple with questions about the lived and diverse reality of religion and worldviews in the world. It explores the diverse ways in which people practise their beliefs. It engages with the impact of beliefs on individuals, communities and societies. Pupils will investigate the ways in which religions and worldviews have shaped and continue to shape societies around the world. This approach can promote better understanding of the ways in which religion and worldviews influence people's understanding of power, gender, compassion, and so on. It also enables pupils to consider the nature of religion itself and the diverse ways in which people understand the term "religion".[26]

We might begin to analyse the knowledge in religious studies curriculum then along the lines shown in Figure 4.5. However, as we've seen, the makeup of the strands that give the subject its interdisciplinary nature is contested, and indeed the way these strands structure substantive knowledge is itself the subject of debate.[27] However, here we have a starting point for discussion.

Knowledge in religious studies can be understood as having a moderate semantic gravity, with fundamental texts, theories, and concepts, and a fairly tall ontological architecture in which applications of beliefs and methods of argument to practices and conclusions sits under these abstract planes, while the concrete details and context-specific cases reflect the human and irreducible nature of belief and its manifestations. For example, the concept of the Trinity in Christianity is highly cerebral, abstract, and challenging, and is interpreted to inform practice in worship, relationships, and power structures by Christian thinkers. However, the integration is weak, since interpretation is intrinsic and underdetermined, and making meaning tends to follow an accumulative or more often discursive epistemology. Thus, work in the field of production of religious studies tends to take the form of essays offering an interpretation or argument and in school curriculum we

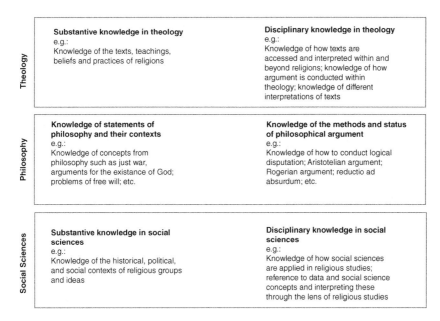

Figure 4.5 Knowledge in religious studies curriculum

seek to build the components of this writing, and their synthesis into full pieces. The distinction, often seen in the assessment in religious studies, between *learning about religion* and *learning from religion* can be understood as reflecting the different spheres of knowledge in religious studies, in the particulars, both abstract and concrete, of religions (knowledge about religions) and the discussion of the interpretations of these teachings, in the world of individuals and groups (knowledge from religion).[28]

The knowledge in religious studies is densely linked, with areas across religions and across the disciplinary strands having causal and comparative relations. It is not highly necessary in its manthanology however, and sequencing typically can follow many diverse routes, each collectively sufficient. Progression manifests in an expanding domain of substantive knowledge, as well as in an ascending quality of student responses, drawing on an increasing number of techniques as well as the developing quality of discursive writing itself.

Questions for discussion

- What is the purpose of the religious studies curriculum? What are the changes it is intended to effect in its students? What content can constitute collective sufficiency for this goal?

- If the school is bound to a Local Agreement, what are its particulars? How might we interpret these?

- Which disciplines should be reflected in the curriculum? What are the characteristics of each strand? What should be the balance of these strands?

- Which religions and worldviews should be studied, and why?

- What are the key ideas and concrete details that should be included, and what are their roles?

- What does it mean to get better at each of the disciplinary strands? What are the components of excellent work in these strands? Where are these components explicitly taught and practised?

- What considerations should there be for sequencing? What needs to be understood first in order to access X? What knowledge can offer collective sufficiency for accessing X? What details can bring richness of understanding to later work?

Languages

To be able to communicate in a second language is a wonderful thing. To be able to shift between one's native language and a second, to understand and to find oneself understood, holds not just utility but also fascination and delight. Knowing, and living-in, a foreign language brings us insights into human existence, the logic, structure, and features of language, and concepts of meaning and representations. Through languages we truly travel out of ourselves; there is joy in our ability to express and interpret meaning across linguistic and geographical divides. There is logic in languages but also character and expression. Languages evoke. Our interactions with languages are personal and involve us acutely as subjects. When we live-in languages, we live another life.

Languages are quasi-natural phenomena: systems and structures that have arisen over time, out of the combination of physiological, psychological, and anthropological factors in human history. They are a species-wide, universal constant of human culture. Part of the study of languages is a sort of meta-study of the phenomena, uncovering the hidden rules that govern them, exploring the highways and winding roads of etymology and morphology, and all that they reveal. Arguably though, in school languages, these explications are present only as servants of the primary goals of language curriculum: those of acquisition, fluency, and accuracy. In school languages the aim is ultimately to learn the language; the curriculum is the language itself, built meaningfully over time. The successful speaking, listening, reading, and writing of the target language, and the ability to live-in the language with authenticity, are the desired outcomes of the curriculum, with formal linguistic elements playing an interesting and important – but ultimately secondary – role.

This quasi-natural phenomenon-status of languages lies at the very heart of how languages are learned and of how curriculum should be thought about as a result. Using languages draws on very specific brain regions and cognitive structures[29] and learning a language as a native speaker has been shown to be a biologically primary rather than secondary activity.[30] It has been shown that students learn languages better in chunks of association, with practised flexibility rather than in fixed and isolated parts,[31] and that repeated practice, while important for all learning, is critical in large amounts to language acquisition.[32] While native speakers do not need to receive explicit syntax or morphology instruction in order for them to speak fluently, for the child receiving two or three lessons a week plus homework, making the rules of the language explicit provides a powerful shortcut to understanding and fluency, and is therefore a key curricular component.

One way of characterising the knowledge in language curriculum is shown in Figure 4.6. A language can be analysed into component parts: vocabulary and

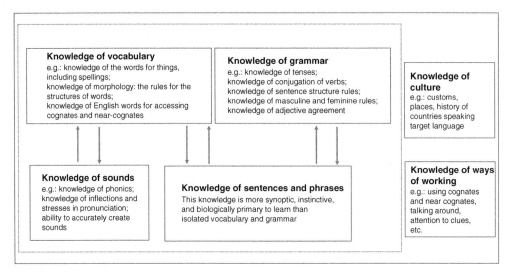

Figure 4.6 Knowledge in languages curriculum

grammar, or words and rules. However, due to the physiological and cognitive factors discussed above, it seems that languages are held in our memories in larger pieces: sentences and phrases that chunk together several words and syntactic and morphological rules. This is significant because an over-reductive interpretation of the knowledge in languages can have damaging implications for curriculum planning and pedagogy. This chunking is therefore represented as a distinct category in Figure 4.6, with the aim of showing the essential resistance to reduction at the heart of the uniquely *cognitive* ontology of languages. Indeed, teachers of languages often find that there is a marked overlap, more than for many other subjects, between planning curriculum and planning pedagogy, and this is perhaps a reflection of the biologically primary origins of the object of study itself, the deep and old connections between brain and language.

Sounds in a language are a fundamental part of the knowledge structure too: both the physical skill of creating the right sounds and the knowledge of how sounds relate to spellings on the page, known in the subject discourse as phonics (or phonological awareness.) Again, this knowledge is at once both a discrete component and highly interconnected, in particular to knowledge of vocabulary. The four areas of knowledge: of words, grammar, phrases, and sounds are linked together and feed into one another; knowledge of phrases includes and is built by explicit grammar and isolated vocabulary; knowledge of words is closely linked to knowledge of sounds, both in the connections of meanings to sounds, and in the movement from notation to sounds, and back again. In this way we can see how the four traditional pillars of assessment in languages – the modes of production and reception – namely listening, speaking, reading, and writing, emerge from the knowledge in the subject.[33]

Alongside all of this knowledge-of-language are two other areas that are important, though not directly about the language itself. While it is possible to learn a language without learning about the culture of the places where it is spoken, this would arguably mean an impoverished curriculum and a disadvantaged learner, as culture is so often an assumed component of communication. Facts about rules, customs, geography, and history of a place are all part of the substance of conversations and texts of a language. As comprehension is always a knowledge test to some extent,[34] cultural knowledge is often crucial to understanding, as well of course as having value in its own right in broadening our children's horizons.

This knowledge has a moderate semantic gravity, since the structures of syntax and morphology are abstract and transcendent, being applicable to many situations and not tied to any context, while on the other hand the particulars of vocabulary and sentence structure are crucial, and increasing knowledge of the language comprises increasing knowledge of those particulars, rather than just an increasingly deep understanding of the abstract aspects of the language.

Finally, we come to what we might understand as the disciplinary element of languages as a school subject: our ways of working within the language. Techniques such as intentional use of cognates and near-cognates, habits of listening, and so on, are extremely useful and are a feature of proficient language use; these habits can be explicitly taught and should be considered a concrete part of the curriculum.

Typically, there is little or nothing in language curriculum regarding how new knowledge or meaning is generated in the subject discipline, as there is for most other subjects. This reflects an interesting fact about languages: while languages evolve, and people do study them and related areas at high levels of disciplinary work, this work is far removed from the acquisition of the language which is the overarching aim of the school subject. We might say that the recontextualisation of the subject is so significant that the ways of working in the field of production are not meaningful or relevant in school: while students do study some aspects of syntax, morphology, and so on that have been uncovered by specialist workers in the universities and elsewhere, to learn about the ways of working that lead to this knowledge would not lend a great deal to the curriculum, although this is not *a priori* true and may lead to an interesting discussion elsewhere within specialist discourse.

The manthanology of knowledge in language curriculum is not straightforward. It could be argued that knowledge of phonics is largely prior and should be mastered before many other things, since so much practice is done through speaking and listening, and the role of the internal voice is also a significant cognitive entity in reading and writing, though this area warrants further research.[35] There are also aspects of grammar such as gender agreement and conjugations that allow a great deal to be accessed once they have been grasped, and the numerous "high-frequency" sentence structures and vocabulary can provide a strong foundation if learned early on. Beyond these moderate-necessity areas, much of the knowledge can follow a sufficiency-model, with various routes possible for meaningful progression through the curriculum. Often more important than sequencing of material *per se* is the cycling back through previous material alongside new, providing the practice that this very wide and detailed knowledge structure insists on for effective acquisition.

Questions for discussion

■ How should the curriculum be structured to build memory of the very broad and detailed domain?

■ What are the sentence structures that students should learn? How should they be mapped for introduction and repeated practice throughout?

■ What high-frequency vocabulary should the curriculum develop? What specialist vocabulary should be introduced and when?

■ How should students be taught to combine what they have learned to produce and interpret new material?

■ How should phonics and other aspects of pronunciation feature in curriculum?

■ How should the curriculum develop students' ways of working as linguists?

■ How should culture feature in the curriculum?

Art

We turn now from the largely descriptive and interpretive quests to the more expressive, beginning with art. The intentional making of marks or shaping of material to create something with significance is one of the oldest human activities, as the paintings on the walls of the caves which once housed our ancestors attest. It is quite breath-taking to be able to look at these marks, thousands of years later, and experience the same meaning (possibly) as their creator intended: to see an ox, horse, or hunter, brought from nothing by a hand thousands of years earlier. Since then and throughout our history, art has sought variously to record, to evoke, to worship, to flatter, to depict, and to express – but running through all of these is the making of meaning for the artist and/or the viewer, through the choice, arrangement and execution of visual elements. This is the central quest of art.

As a school subject, art has several facets: it seeks to develop students' understanding and appreciation of art, and of art history, as well as seeking to develop their ability to produce art themselves. These subject strands link to three fields of production: art criticism, the history of art, and the work of practising artists.

Figure 4.7 shows how we might conceive of the knowledge in art curriculum. The distinction between substantive and disciplinary knowledge is probably less useful in art since it tends to be conceived of as a practical subject with the quest embodied in creative products rather than claims about the world. The areas explicated above fit more readily into the traditional strands of theory and practical, though it is clear that there is significant overlap and reciprocity between the areas.

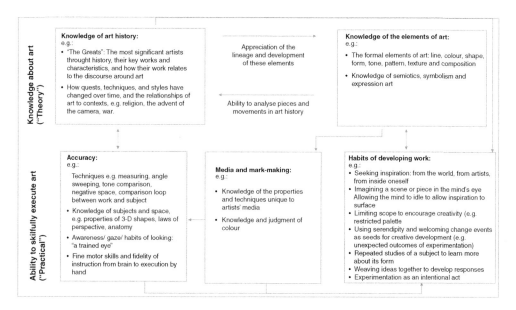

Figure 4.7 Knowledge in art curriculum

Beginning with knowledge for practical execution of art then, we can see three distinct (though linked) areas, starting with what has been termed here "accuracy". Proficient artists draw upon measurement and judgment techniques, explicit knowledge of rules and principles such as those of perspective and anatomy; tacit awareness and habits of looking and noticing, the physiological sensitivities of their fine motor skills in their hands and their ability to realise the signals from their brain into precise movements. Such knowledge is at the heart of excellent work in art, though it has often been overlooked in curriculum. While some students bring a natural ability in accuracy to the subject, these components are teachable to all,[36] and even the most proficient of students will benefit from developing this knowledge further.

Knowledge of how to use the media of the artist, of the techniques for pencil, charcoal, oil pastels, acrylic and watercolour paint, for example, are all components of the knowledge in art. Theory of colour and proficiency in mixing and judgement are another significant practical component. These areas have been grouped here under "media and mark-making".

Habits of developing work are the final component to the practical knowledge in art, and these habits draw upon the elements of accuracy and use of media already discussed, as well as the areas of theory represented in the top section of the graphic. These habits of development comprise several components, and can build towards a single, developed "final piece" although that is not to say that they always must do so.

Moving now to the more theory-oriented areas of knowledge in art, we come to knowledge of the formal elements of art and of semiotics. Knowledge of these elements gives students a language that allows them to analyse their own work, receive and understand precise instruction and feedback, and to participate in rewarding analysis and appreciation of the work of great artists throughout history.[37] As such, knowledge of these elements of art enhances students' experience and work both in their practical execution of art and in art history. Here we find knowledge of the great masters throughout history, their key works and characteristics, and their significance in their context and in the development of art and its discourse. An understanding of the elements and developments of this discourse, such as the changing prominences of verisimilitude versus personal expression, is an important overarching strand in this area of curriculum. Knowledge of art history can inform and inspire students' practical work, which in turn allows greater appreciation of the work of artists over time, since students have practically participated in this "great conversation" in their own drawing, painting, and so on.

These areas of knowledge are highly interlinked and reciprocal. The development of one area is often fed by, and can, in turn feed others. All must be developed in order for authentic progression to be realised. As such, art has a moderate semantic gravity, with large amounts of fairly esoteric theory in terms of semiotics and the formal elements of art, as well as intermediate-gravity theory of things such as perspective and anatomy, all the while very much tied to context in that the piece of art itself, and not just the principles behind it, is the thing of importance. Ontologically, we find a moderately tall architecture in art, with fundamental principles of theory and practical invocations as just mentioned. New meaning is added to the field by the production of works, and these are accumulative or discursive, adding to the conversation, building a movement, answering a call; attendant to this epistemology are many interpretations and lenses that can feed into curricular work.

Manthanologically there are several considerations to be made. The habits of development of work are composite, drawing upon all other areas of knowledge, with obvious implications for sequencing. Accuracy should inform use of media and mark-making, and the components of accuracy can be usefully contextualised in the history of art. This is not to say that art curriculum should move exclusively from accuracy early on to exclusively media and mark-making later on, but that the continued development of accuracy must be an explicit component throughout if authentic progression is to be achieved. It can certainly be argued that basics of observational drawing, measurement, perspective, portraiture and anatomy must be in place before any meaningful development of ideas can be engaged in.[38]

Questions for discussion

- How should the curriculum develop students' accuracy?

- What exercises can build students' abilities in observation, mark-making, use of colour and media?

- How should the curriculum develop students' habits of developing ideas?

- How should ideas about the formal elements of art, art history and semiotics be developed throughout the curriculum?

- How should the curriculum structure students' learning from art history in their own practical work?

Music

As in art, in music we find meaning through the creative arrangement of components, expressing something on the part of the maker, evoking something in the experience of the engaged, seeking beauty or some other aesthetic property emergent from creation. Where art deals in light, music deals in sound; colours are in many ways analogous to notes; composition is key to both. Some comparisons with art can help us to uncover the nature of music further.

While a piece of art presents itself all at once, a work in space whose parts may be simultaneously apprehended by the viewer, music unfolds over time, with a sequence of components and an order of things. This necessary linearity and *durée* is a function of the medium, and is intrinsic to the experience of music as listeners, appreciators, performers, and composers.

In the section on art we considered the role of accuracy, both in the execution of work, and in the relationship with the world in figurative work: how apparent angles, lengths, and tones need to correspond between world and page, so that a person or knower may experience meaning and verisimilitude. In music, too, accuracy in execution is key, and there are many pieces of music that emulate the world, emulating the rises and falls of a bird's call, the rolling of thunder, the marching of armies. And just as art is at once both less and more than photography, so is this figurative music both less and more than a recording: the composer's and player's flourishes, emphases and omissions bring the interpretivist and expressivist strands that make this work appealing, memorable and at times, intensely personal. Unlike art, in music we usually have two distinct levels of skill, interpretation and expression: once in the composition of a piece, and then in its performance by a musician or musicians, and each of these is a creator of meaning.

Music seems to uncover truth, or to create meaning and beauty, not by showing something, but by the relations of its parts as it progresses through time:

> The sequence of sounds that you hear at the start of Beethoven's Third Piano Concerto are not heard simply as a sequence. They contain a movement, and this movement is in musical space. It is not movement of the kind you observe in machines or even in animals. It is an expression of an intention – the intention contained in the music (which is not necessarily a private intention of the composer's). Put another way, this is a movement of which you can, at any point, ask "why?" Why, for example, does it descend stepwise from the G, having got there by a leaping arpeggio? Why, having got back to the starting point, does it proceed to emphasise its being there with two dominant to tonic punctuation marks? You might find these questions difficult to answer. But they make sense, just as though they were asked of human actions […] The whole theme unfolds

through questions and answers, like a game of chess, and this gives substance to the widespread feeling that a work like this is saying something – though not something that could be put into words.[39]

The meaning in music seems to be derived from the experience of intention, the being brought-along by a piece, and the experience of each consecutive development being *right*, both with regard to its immediate predecessor and to the piece as a whole; and of the feeling of a reaction to the music, whether a nameable emotion or just an appreciation of the piece, that is felt to be a product of the intention of the composer and performer/s, and likely shared by other listeners. In hearing music, written and played with this intensely *human* intention, we meet and delight in Husserl's *Lebenswelt*.

In music curriculum we find the opportunity for students to join the conversations that have taken place between composer, performer, listener-self and listener-companion, for hundreds, even thousands of years. To be able to appreciate, articulate, and participate in the triumphs of musical prowess across the world and the ages is, ultimately, the aim of music curriculum, and its realisation for all is contingent on the bringing of students into the language, concepts, and codes of practical music and theory, and their manifestations in the notational world.

Newcomers to music are often surprised to learn of its deeply mathematical nature. While art engages with space, which is undoubtedly subject to mathematical interpretation, and often makes use of mathematics in aspects such as composition and colour, this is often (though not always) instinctive on the part of the artist, and is not always or even often a necessary explicit framework for the success of art. In music, however, the reverse is true. Music exists in time across a linear progression, and this line is navigated through counting, either implicit or explicit. Rhythms are fractions in time. The relations of notes to each other, in tones, keys, chords, and scales, are governed by mathematics, and the developments, reflections, and responses across a piece of music are all both made of mathematical materials, and set against a mathematical backdrop, like an embroidery in time where both thread and canvas are made of the same geometric stuff.

Like mathematics, music has its own sophisticated notation. Musical notation facilitates several vital things in music. It allows musical relationships, such as scales, harmonics, and chords to be made explicit and easily discussable. It makes possible the expression and communication of music by one person so that it may be played by another, or indeed many others, and indeed complicated and multi-instrument compositions are largely possible only through the use of musical notation. The ability to read music allows the performer to access and play any piece of music that has been written down; furthermore it facilitates a swifter acquisition of unwritten music, since the musician has trained in articulating the patterns and components of music, and can more rapidly identify and recall them from a new piece.[40] The interpretive, expressive, and creative elements of musical performance are also strengthened in this way, since players simply have more time to develop them, having quickly mastered the essential piece.

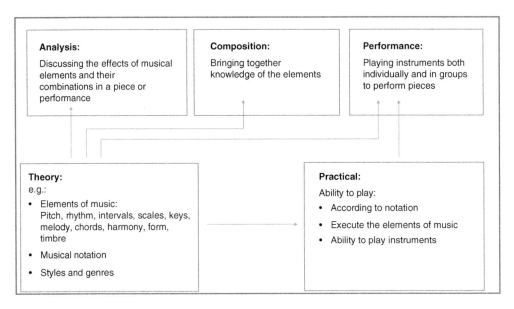

Figure 4.8 Knowledge in music curriculum

One way of considering the knowledge in music curriculum is illustrated in Figure 4.8.[41] Progression in music is often mapped in each of the three areas of performance, analysis, and composition, and these are linked to the two spheres of theory and practical knowledge. Within musical experience, it is very difficult to take full advantage of the meaning and power of the elements of music without an understanding of the notation of music and a lexicon for its components and patterns – and progress in practical music is fed by an understanding of both. Regarding composition and creative work, theory affords the student a more powerful palette to use – a language to articulate how parts might relate to each other and to the whole. For these reasons, music theory can be seen as a strand of fundamental importance, in thinking both about components of progression and about the sequence of components.[42]

The knowledge[43] in music can be understood as having a moderate semantic gravity, in that both abstract theory and the particulars of pieces are both sought and valued by the discipline. The ontology of music theory is very tall, with concepts on many different planes, and core building blocks combining in ever-increasing levels of complexity over many levels. The concept of musical form, for example, "the arrangement of musical units of rhythm, melody, and/or harmony that show repetition or variation, the arrangement of the instruments (as in the order of solos in a jazz or bluegrass performance), or the way a symphonic piece is orchestrated,"[44] among other factors, is contingent on knowledge of musical phrases, which is itself contingent on knowledge of rhythm, melody, and harmony, which are themselves contingent on knowledge of many components such as beats, bars, sharps, flats, and sequences. Thus there is a sharply ascending architecture of meaning and significant implications for the sequencing of curriculum, since there is a great deal of manthanological necessity therein.

In addition, the ontology of music as a whole is very wide, since at every level there are a great many workings, examples, inclusions, and developments of musical concepts and components, in instruments, pieces, genres, and their relations.

The manthanological necessity we find in music theory is a reflection of a strong integration of much of the knowledge therein, and this is an interesting contrast to the creative and expressive field of production of music, where practitioners operate using this highly integrated body of knowledge, to produce new music in an accumulative, contributive, epistemological pattern. It is of course the case that many music practitioners can and do perform without having learnt explicit music theory or notation, but this is perhaps comparable to the engineering feats of ancient civilisations who had no knowledge of the underlying science: when that theory is shared, the knower is empowered in ways of seeing, speed of access, and transfer of ability in ways that simply cannot be achieved in the absence of theory.

Implicit in the practical elements of music curriculum is the importance of practice, of both component parts and larger pieces, in order to develop proficiency and skill. The sequencing of this practice is another key consideration for the structuring of music curriculum, since over time students can develop abilities through practice that can allow rapid access to interesting and ambitious new work, if sequencing is well-planned.

In combining these considerations, music curriculum can bring students into the world of appreciation, sharing, performance, and expression, which are uniquely combined and manifest in music.

Questions for discussion

■ What are the components of music theory that students need to learn?

■ What are the necessary prior components for X?

■ What is a meaningful sequence for these to be taught in?

■ What practical work can help students understand the components of music theory?

■ What are the components of successful practical work?

■ What is a meaningful sequence for them to be taught in?

■ What do students need to learn in order to engage in expressive composition?

■ How can students be shown, and practise, the subjectivist and interpretivist elements of the playing of written music?

■ What great works should be included in music curriculum? What knowledge can they help to build or illustrate for students?

English

Humans have language, and with language we make text, and texts make meaning. Of all the human cultural pursuits, literature, above all others, deals with the human condition: with love and loyalty, rage and betrayal; with irony, personality, and wit; with the sheer joy of the curve of a lover's cheek or the sensation of rich soil beneath one's boots on an autumn walk. All of these things are so real to us, and when they are articulated by master writers we both experience recognition and our awareness of our own experience is heightened. We reflect, and we are connected in the world by knowing that others share our experiences too. If geography covers everything on the Earth, literature covers everything in the Self.

Literature is typically defined as artistic works in language: plays, poetry, and stories. Other forms of writing are important too: speeches, reporting, and factual writing. These are usually referred to as transactional writing (writing intended to communicate information), and along with literature form a significant part of the objects of study in English. The examination distinction between "literature" and "language" in part reflects these two spheres of study in English, but two other important spheres overarch both and mean that arguably, in curricular thinking, a separation of the two is often a distraction. First of these overarching strands is the mechanics and effects of language: its syntax, semantics, and morphology, but also its evocations, connotations, and flavours. Rules and feelings alike have a bearing on both artistic and informative writing. Second is the development of students' own ability in language: in English, students respond in the same medium as their object of study, producing composition in English to analyse, explore, and show understanding of the literary and transactional pieces under consideration. In both language and literature, students' ability to write well is fundamental.

Texts can be studied, analysed, discussed, and interpreted. This study of the meaning in texts, and of how to produce texts with meaning and elegance – *to wit*, to write well – are the quests of English as a subject. There are several strands to this quest. In areas such as the study of grammar, we find a descriptivist quest; in textual analysis we see an interpretivist quest. In creative writing we are expressive and in transactional writing we are solving-producing. English is, paradoxically, both an intrinsically hybrid and a highly specialist subject. In this subject we draw on many, many domains and pursue many quests, but it is not always or even often interdisciplinary in the way that religious studies is. Rather, it is at once integrative and emergent. English is simultaneously many things and something unique.

English has something of a reputation for being hard to pin down, since it is highly diverse, interlinked, integrated, holistic, and unbounded. Attempts to compartmentalise or itemise knowledge in English carry the danger of leading to damaging, reductive effects because they can miss or distort the intrinsic anarchy of

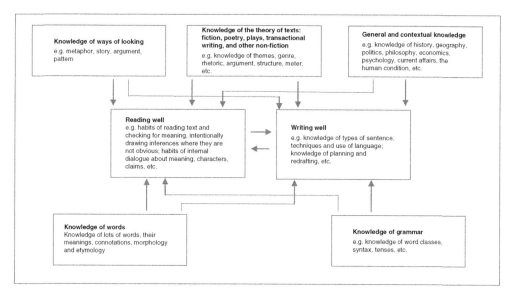

Figure 4.9 Knowledge in English curriculum

knowledge in the subject. However, it is possible to begin to identify the main components of knowledge within English, and one approach to doing so is shown in Figure 4.9.

This knowledge is extremely densely linked: knowledge of a specific text, for example, will draw heavily on students' knowledge of literature theory, vocabulary, grammar, and general knowledge; while a student's writing or reading on a topic could potentially draw on all of the areas identified here.[45] This knowledge has a flattish ontology: while there are abstract ideas such as themes and literary devices, these are not hierarchically above other areas of knowledge in any organising sense. The integration is weak, since there are multiple interpretations of the links between areas: knowledge about the context of a piece, for example, could enhance a person's ability to write a powerful analysis of that piece, but precisely what knowledge and the details of the enhancement are not clear, and many permutations are possible.[46]

Substantive knowledge in English can be understood to include knowledge of literary texts and traditions, vocabulary, etymology, morphology, and syntax, and claims about literature and language made by theorists in those specialisms. David Didau's suggestion of "ways of looking": metaphor, story, argument, and pattern,[47] is a powerful insight into the types of meaning that we make when experiencing and analysing literature and other text, and a useful heuristic for developing processes and habits in students. The disciplinary strand can be characterised as comprising the habits and approaches "with which students can ask questions of the claims made by others and frame their own responses to the substantive knowledge they encounter",[48] including analogising, and *noticing*: "reading and writing whilst being attuned to the choices and effects of everything that language has to offer: punctuation, sounds, diction, syntax, patterns of form, imagery and the ways each of these combines to make narratives and arguments".[49]

Progression in English can be analysed as existing in all the areas identified above, with important curriculum thinking being done in the field around the components of this progression and their sequencing.[50] There is often a surprising degree of necessity in the manthanology of knowledge in English, with components such as using tentative language and making links across a text, if not quite keys to otherwise unopenable doors, very powerful antecedents to challenging work in English curriculum, and certainly worthy of careful attention. Typically though, sequencing will often also attend to narrative, interweaving, and synthesis, as ideas are developed and returned to, and skills built and brought together across the curriculum.

Questions for discussion

- What are the details of the knowledge strands outlined above, and how can they be mapped, explicitly taught, practised, and brought together across the curriculum?

- What are the types of texts we want students to experience in this curriculum? Why? Which texts early on can build readiness for later texts - in themes, style, or language?

- What are the components of excellent analysis and writing? How should these be mapped in the curriculum?

- What vocabulary and contextual knowledge can build students' understanding and appreciation in a meaningful way? How should these be sequenced with other, related knowledge?

- What understandings of language will build students' appreciation and ability? How should this knowledge be developed throughout the curriculum?

Physical education

No cultural area has greater power to inspire, excite, and unite than that manifest in sport. In sport we find an intoxicating mixture of personal physical prowess, born of dedicated training and preparation; of rules and constraints creating structures for an endeavour to be pursued; of chance and unpredictability; the thrill of the competition; the hanging of tantalising possibilities in the air; the emotion of winners and losers. This drama is played out at the interface between spheres: the physical bodies and the intangible selves of the competitors, with their personal living-in the sport, and the physical backdrop and rules of the sport itself – all in existence along an acute temporal line, where "before" and "after" carry all the meaning – where victory is claimed and fates sealed.

Along this critical timeline, participant and spectator alike derive meaning from performance: a skilled execution, a wise anticipation of play, an adept response to a sudden challenge; all of these delight and in doing so constitute the making of meaning in sport.

Accompanying this huge cultural endeavour is a body of attendant theoretical knowledge: associated anatomy, physiology, psychology, and other theory. Physical education is partly a recontextualisation of sport and these associated specialisms. The gaze in sport is one of personal commitment, focus, competition, personal betterment and deference to structures in rules and traditions; in physical education we find this gaze and also the factual, problem-solving, applied empirical gaze of the sports sciences.[51]

Physical education is unique among the school subjects in that one of its main, explicit goals is participation[52] in addition to the knowledge in the curriculum. This participation is an object in itself, both for the immediate benefits to students' health and well-being, and for the building of lifelong habits in sports and exercise.

Figure 4.10 presents a model to interpret PE curriculum, representing both the knowledge and the participation contained therein.

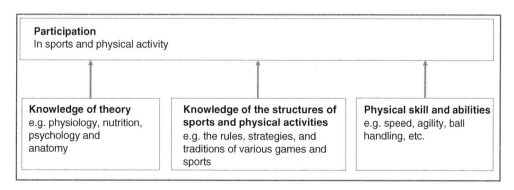

Figure 4.10 Knowledge in PE curriculum

Feeding into and fed by participation are three strands of knowledge in PE. Knowledge of the theory and structures of PE is largely declarative knowledge, while skills and abilities are almost entirely non-declarative or procedural and often largely tacit, with implications for curriculum design.

The development of these strands in curriculum should therefore be informed by these differences, and the components of progression in these strands planned and mapped accordingly. Manthanologically, there is a necessity of components before wholes, particularly with team sports or performances (as opposed to athletics), but between activities there is little directionality, with most sports being flexible in terms of curricular order.

Questions for discussion

■ Which competitive sports should be included in the physical education curriculum?

■ What conditions need to prevail in order for all students to participate in authentic, well-matched competition?

■ What non-competitive physical activities should be included in the curriculum?

■ What are the components of PE theory that should be developed in PE curriculum?

■ For each sport or physical activity, what are the components of knowledge of structures, such as game rules and regulations, that students should learn?

■ For each sport or physical activity, what are the components of the development of the desired physical abilities and skills? What drills and exercises can help all students to develop in these areas?

■ How should the PE curriculum support students in bringing together component skills into composite performance?

Design and technology

In the list of cultural areas that define our humanity, technology is surely one of the headliners. The ability to use tools and materials to make things and change the environment has given us the evolutionary success, the resources, the time and the freedom to develop as a species with culture. It is no exaggeration to say that without technology, none of our other disciplines would exist. Many other species change their environment: birds' nests, beavers' dams and termite mounds are all examples of the extended phenotype[53]; and several groups such as some apes and birds use primitive tools, but in humans the level of this practice is on a staggering scale. That scale is a result of the cumulative body of knowledge in technology: the ideas, theory, and principles that allow intentional, developmental, integrative, and complex design, far beyond trial and error and rudimentary production.

In a sense, anything that we have made that is physical and useful rather than purely aesthetic can be included under the term of design and technology: architecture, engineering, furniture design, home appliances, fashion, and so on. Work in design and technology is often characterised as "problem-solving", where the term "problem" is often used to denote an opportunity rather than a negative. Products are desirable in part because they do something useful, but they also have value beyond the functional; they are ergonomic and aesthetic. Physical objects, of course, can be seen, and so designers attend to the appearance of a product as well as its utility. Designers communicate ideas and create experiences in the user and the viewer through the appearance of products: the materials, angles, compositions, and colours of things are variously tailored to be beautiful, impressive, slick, nonchalant, imposing, understated, or flamboyant, to name but a few of these design expressions.

There is a drama to design and technology: with a setting in the field of human activity, a problem or opportunity that must be identified, analysed, and solved, characters in the materials and techniques available, and the designer as protagonist. This drama can be understood as comprising two quests: the first is to create product-solutions: objects such as furniture, toys, and appliances that perform a physical function in the lives of people. There are restrictions that govern what outcomes are possible: the materials, components, and physical laws in the world, economic, social, and environmental pressures. The second quest is to express qualities or *qualia* through form: to design the appearance (and texture, haptics and so on) of products in order to provoke certain responses in the user or viewer, and to make meaning in this interaction.

The knowledge in technology can be understood as occupying the areas shown in Figure 4.11.

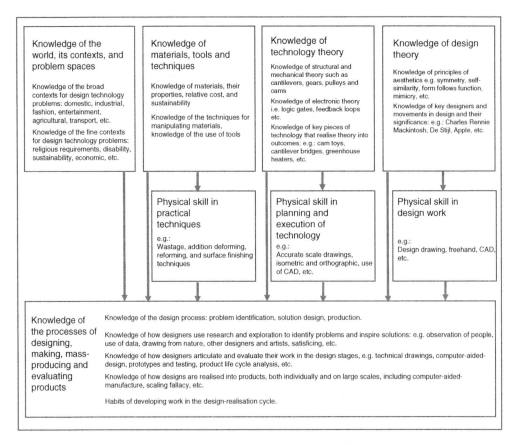

Figure 4.11 Knowledge in design and technology curriculum[54]

As participants in the solving-producing quest of design and technology, students must draw on knowledge of both context and resources in materials, processes, and laws. They might consider the contexts of minimalist interior design, the properties and processes of various woods and their manipulations, and the combinations of these factors in furniture design and production.[55] There are also bodies of knowledge in theory of both technology and design which furnish and feed the work of the designer-technologist, such as balance and alignment, repetition, and form-follows-function.[56] These strands can be applied in the practical elements of design and technology, detailed in Figure 4.11 above.[57]

The synthesis of all of this knowledge into the design-realisation cycle is one of the core aims of most technology curricula. As we can see in Figure 4.11, this aspect of knowledge is shown to have both declarative components in relation to the disciplinary field, and habits of developing work executed by the student themselves. This integrative work is highly contingent on each of its components, with significant implications for the sequencing of the knowledge in technology curriculum. Thus project work can often provide a meaningful structure for the components of knowledge laid out above, with students emulating the design realisation cycle of responding to context, creating a design to bring together specific materials, techniques, and theory, and then executing its production according to the specification.

The use of mathematics to analyse both contexts such as details from the sphere of consumers, to the particulars of a design or its execution, is an important element in design and technology, and warrants consideration in curriculum work.

The knowledge in design technology is therefore of moderate semantic gravity, with a great deal of its meaning tied to contexts such as materials, products, and users, but with an equally significant body of rarefied theory such as the principles of design and the cycle of realisation, which are context-independent and transcendent. The ontological architecture is correspondingly flattish, with some abstract principles but not a clear hierarchy between them and other aspects of knowledge in the subject. The manthanology in design technology is broadly one of collective sufficiency, where several alternative routes and sets of components can prepare students for later learning; some flexibility in sequencing can be derived therefrom. It is in the relations – between context, materials, processes and principles, and the final product – that significant meaning is made, though the particulars and details of those components are also significant curricular objects, worthy of careful attention and detailed codification.[58]

Questions for discussion

- What knowledge of contexts, materials, techniques, product types, and iconic designs should be present in the technology curriculum?

- What principles of design should be included?

- What practical skills should be taught? How should these be related to other strands of knowledge in order for meaning to be made?

- What are the elements of mathematics in the curriculum? How should they be mapped for progression and meaning?

- What elements of the design-realisation cycle can allow the synthesis of components of design and technology curriculum? How should students be taught to combine context, problem, materials, techniques, and design principles into the plans and production of effective work?

- To what extent should students be able to articulate their thinking in speech, drawing and in writing? What are the components of excellence in this speech, drawing and writing? How should these components feature in the curriculum?

- What should the role of project work be in design technology curriculum?

Food

We turn now to the cousin of design and technology, and another solving-producing-aesthetic quest: food. The preparation of food, in particular its cooking and presentation, is unique to our species, and it is worth reflecting on the significance of this. Anthropologists have argued that the development of cooking technology was pivotal in human cognitive and cultural development, since it meant early humans were able to take more energy from their food, freeing up time and also providing the increase in energy demanded by increasingly large brains.[59] Food, then, is at the centre of our history and development, as well as being key to so much of contemporary culture, celebration, and everyday life.

In food, we find a similar combination of quests to that in design technology. Dishes can be seen as products and solutions, fulfilling desires for taste, texture and nutritional value, and being a conduit of expression, celebration, and meaning, made manifest through physical form. Again, the theory, tools, and techniques sitting behind food design and production are a significant and rarefied body of knowledge, one that joyfully brings meaning into the world both for the proficient cook and for the diner.

We can understand the knowledge in food as comprising the areas denoted in Figure 4.12. In the integrative abilities to cook, students must draw on knowledge of nutrition, health, and dietary requirements, equipment and techniques, and the characteristics of ingredients. Knowledge of recipes can be understood on two scales: the proficient cook has knowledge both of complete and detailed recipes but also of the components or principles that make up recipes: concepts such as bases, seasoning, balance, contrast and so on. There are significant links between

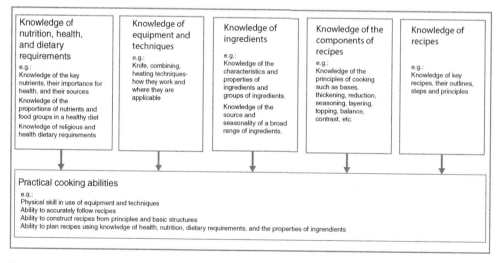

Figure 4.12 Knowledge in food curriculum

these areas of course, since, for example, particular ingredients are associated with particular techniques, forming sub-components of particular recipe components, and so on. The ontology is flattish, with some abstract principles but significance tied to the details of individual dishes. There is largely collective-sufficiency manthanology, although there are broadly agreed fundamentals, such as food hygiene, chopping techniques, and so on that would typically precede other components for effective progression.

Questions for discussion

- What are the components of knowledge in the four strands that the curriculum should develop?

- What recipes will allow students to practise and bring together the components of knowledge?

- How should recipes be sequenced to introduce, integrate, and practise these components?

- Which components should be taught outside of recipes, for efficiency and/or meaning?

Computing

The development of computing and computer science is undoubtedly one of the great intellectual and technological triumphs of human endeavour, and has utterly transformed the social, cultural, and economic landscapes of our time. The advances in related technology, the changes to quality of life, the implications for so many fields, from science to politics to music, and the democratisation of access to information and communication that computers and the internet have brought, have defined and continue to define a revolution in human history.

Computers are so useful because we can give them inputs and get desired outputs, as when we search a term, type an essay, complete a calculation, or edit a photo. At the fundamental, physical level, computers are made of millions of tiny switches called transistors. As electrical current flows through these switches, they turn off and on in patterns that carry messages, in a similar way to patterns of ink on a page carrying message in written letters. There are only two characters in the computer though, and we call them 0 (off) and 1 (on). This is binary code.

The input to the computer (such as a digital photo), the output (edited photo), and the processing (change the colours if the filter button is pressed) are all expressed in binary code within the computer. The computer understands binary code, but for humans it is very difficult, because the combinations of 0s and 1s are hard to remember and interpret.

Computer programs provide an interface between the user and the computer, allowing a translation between a command such as clicking a filter button with a mouse, and the binary code that the computer understands. (Translators such as compilers are needed for this to work.) The instructions within the program cause the desired processing of the input to take place, so that the photo output has a filter effect. Different programs allow different processing, and deal with different types of inputs: some deal with numbers or words, for example.

Computer programs are written in programming languages, such as Java, HTML, or R. Often the first language learnt by students of computing is Python. There are many computing languages because each allows instructions to be written differently, meaning that results can be achieved in a way that best suits the problem, developer and/or hardware. Programming involves the use of an appropriate language, paired with an understanding of the principles of computational thinking: things like logic and structures of algorithms, to plan the series of steps that the computer will go through with each input, in order to process it in the desired way and achieve the output required.

Computing occupies an intersection of spaces in a similar way to design technology. In computing's case, the intersecting planes can be understood as the possibilities of hardware, the principles of computation, and the problem-space of requirements or conceptual possibilities, performing a function either immediately or ultimately for some kind of consumer. At the interface, the capacities – both of programmers and the programming language used – interact with objective possibilities; if they are successful, they produce something that does something useful or desirable. The quest of computing is to achieve things at this intersection, to solve problems and create products that are useful or desirable. The gaze of computing is logical, analytical, pragmatic, problem-solving, experimental, questioning, creative, integrative. In computing, the main questions are usually: "How can we make that work?", "What can we make?" and "What can we add?"

The knowledge in computing can be understood using the areas laid out in Figure 4.13.[60]

In the background, or perhaps overarching, all knowledge in computing is what we might understand as a social sciences and ethics strand, made up of declarative knowledge about the interactions between computers and society. Students learn about the uses of computing, laws governing computing, issues such as security, privacy, and safety. Knowledge of the physical makeup of computers is a distinct strand, and interestingly, although of course linked in-the-world to all other areas of computing, this area of knowledge is not a necessary or even frequently discussed link to the other key areas of knowledge in computing.

The use of information communication technology, or ICT, is a key area of knowledge encompassed in this subject, though it is largely independent of computer science. The use of desktop applications to present ideas, process data, to research and communicate, is self-evidently empowering knowledge, if not exactly power-*ful* in Young's sense, although it is worth noting that in spreadsheet applications

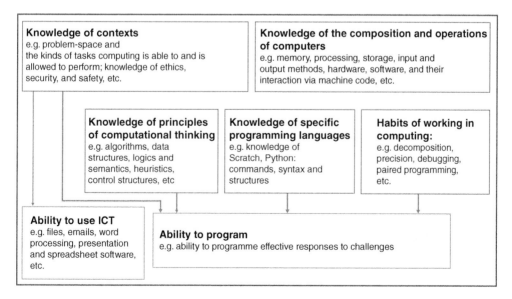

Figure 4.13 Knowledge in computing curriculum

in particular, there are some very sophisticated things that can be achieved, and indeed some links to computing in the programming aspects.

The knowledge in computer science can be understood as having three key strands: the principles of computational thinking, the specifics of individual programming languages, and the habits of working needed for programming, represented in the middle row of Figure 4.13. These strands are integrated into procedural ability or skill in programming, represented at the bottom of the figure.

A great deal of the knowledge in computer science is procedural and composite, and this characteristic has implications for the structuring of curriculum, and the importance of practice, feedback, and project work as well as explicit teaching of components.

It is broadly agreed[61] that the principles and habits of computing are a priority in early computing education, and that languages can be learned later on, having internalised the fundamentals and ways of working at an earlier stage. For this reason, pseudo-code such as Scratch forms a significant part of most school computing curricula, as it allows students to practise both of these more fundamental areas of knowledge without needing to have mastered a programming language. In Scratch, students drag blocks containing commands such as "point towards", "change x to y" and "when x key is pressed" to produce algorithms equivalent to those produced in real programming. This allows feedback in real-time as students can see the outputs produced, and can adapt their algorithms in response. In working in this way they can build their knowledge of the principles of computing, the structures of algorithms and the rules of Boolean logic, and develop the habits of precision, debugging, and problem decomposition so crucial to effective programming. These fundamental things are usually taught explicitly early on, and then returned to or interwoven in each subsequent programming unit.

In progressing through computing curriculum, the expanding domain covers declarative knowledge about computer makeup and computers in society, knowledge of principles and specific programming languages such as Scratch and Python, and increasing levels of skill with these languages and with computational thinking in general. There is a great deal of necessity to the manthanology in computing, with many specific components requiring mastery before other areas can be accessed. The principles of interweaving and semantic waving are also significant to questions of sequencing in computing, as students must learn to combine components of knowledge and transfer principles, structures, and patterns of working.

Questions for discussion

■ What are the components of ICT proficiency that the curriculum should develop? How should these be mapped?

- How should the curriculum develop the components of computational thinking? How should these be brought together in synthesis over time?

- How are students taught effective habits for programming and how are these internalised?

- How should the curriculum develop the movement between concrete situations and algorithms?

- How can the use of pseudo-code support the progression in curriculum?

- How should the curriculum be built in order to develop fluency?

Conclusion to the subjects

In our brief tour of the subjects, we have seen quests, gazes, knowledge structures, and ways of working in staggering variety and diversity. The ability of humans to specialise in so many ways – to make meaning from so many aspects of the world, to interact with it through manifold avenues, to create and describe, to derive sense, utility, beauty, and belonging – should give us pause for reflection and appreciation. Our job in schools, in keeping these specialist fires alight, is a daunting and inspiring one.

At the risk of labouring the point, the analyses are offered as starting points for dialogue around this vitally important area. A non-specialist will find a window onto the specialisms, but not the whole picture. Reading and engagement with the discourse, and ideally with experts open to questions from a novice, will develop understanding of the specialisms further. This understanding should strengthen authentic leadership of diverse subjects across the specialism divide.

Having now explored both the beginnings of curriculum theory and the specialisms themselves, we turn now to the perhaps more prosaic but nonetheless vital task in curriculum work: to the writing-down of things in curriculum, or *codification*.

Notes

1 See DfE (2014)
2 See McCourt (2019): mastery teaching is vital in mathematics due to the highly contingent nature of knowledge upon other knowledge in the domain.
3 See, for example, Sturdy (2017)
4 See DfE (2014)
5 See e.g. Waugh (2000) pp. 2–3
6 See e.g. Clifford (2009)
7 See Maude (2016) for an interesting analysis.
8 See DfE (2014)
9 In conversation with B. Ranson, 2020
10 Counsell (2020) p. 101
11 See e.g. Enser 2019
12 See e.g. Walter (2020)
13 Husbands (1996) p. 4
14 Ibid. p. 5
15 Counsell (2017)
16 See e.g. https://www.history.org.uk/secondary/categories/pp-disciplinary-concepts
17 See Burnage (2019)
18 Woodcock (2005)

19 Riley (2008)
20 See e.g. Burnage (2019)
21 Oldfield et al. (2019)
22 Kueh (2019)
23 Smith (2019)
24 Oldfield et al. (2019) p. 11
25 Ibid. p. 12
26 Ibid. p. 13
27 Kueh (2019)
28 Though the "learning from religion" construct has not been without controversy: see https://core.ac.uk/download/pdf/40033731.pdf p. 191
29 Pinker (1994) p. 45
30 Geary (2013)
31 Baukham (2016) p. 9
32 Lightbrown (2006)
33 Baukham (2016); Conti (2017)
34 Willingham (2010) p. 88
35 Maxwell (2019) p. 44
36 See e.g. Davies (1994)
37 See e.g. Berger (1972)
38 See Blanchflower (2019)
39 Scruton (2014) pp. 144–145
40 Cohen et al. (2011)
41 See Vorderman (2015)
42 John Stevens in conversation.
43 In its broad sense, i.e. the set of schemata we hope to help our students to build.
44 Titon (2009)
45 See Foster (2020)
46 See e.g. Fairclough (1989) Ch. 5
47 Didau (2021) p. 43
48 Ibid.
49 Ibid. p. 43
50 Needham (2019)
51 The epistemology of sport, in relation to refereeing, VAR and so on, is a fascinating area which has been discussed elsewhere, e.g. https://www.bbc.co.uk/programmes/articles/1MTy3sjRmcTrVpjfzh6BbmP/uncertainty-and-var-should-you-embrace-the-unknown
52 See e.g. DfE (2014) and Arnold (1988)
53 See Dawkins (1982)
54 See DfE (2014)
55 Norman et al. (2000) Ch. 7
56 Lidwell et al. (2010)
57 It should be pointed out that the practical elements in design and technology are highly varied and domain specific.
58 See Chapter 5.
59 Wrangham (2009)
60 Wing (2012) and Caldwell et al. (2018)
61 See Wing (2012)

References

Arnold, P. *Education, Movement and the Curriculum.* Lewes: Taylor & Francis, 1988

Baukham, I. Modern Foreign Languages Pedagogy Review, Teaching Schools Council, 2016, available at https://pure.york.ac.uk/portal/files/54043904/MFL_Pedagogy_Review_Report_TSC_PUBLISHED_VERSION_Nov_2016_1_.pdf (accessed 30.12.2019)

Berger, J. *Ways of Seeing.* London: Penguin, 1972

Blanchflower, A. "Knowledge-Rich Y7 Portraiture", Knowledge-Rich Art, 2019, available at https://knowledgerich.art.blog/2019/12/27/knowledge-rich-y7-portraiture/ (accessed 30.12.2019)

Burnage, M. "How Can We Teach Disciplinary Knowledge", In the Name of Rigour, 2019, available at https://inthenameofrigour.wordpress.com/2019/10/10/how-can-we-teach-disciplinary-knowledge/ (accessed 20.12.2019)

Caldwell, H., Pirmann, T., Krotoski, A., Quigley, C. and Foster, P. *Help Your Kids With Computer Science.* New York: Dorling Kindersley, 2018

Clifford, N. "Globalisation: Science, (Physical) Geography and Environment" in N. Clifford, S. Holloway, S. Rice, and G. Valentine (Eds.), *Key Concepts in Geography.* London: Sage, 2009

Cohen, M.A., Evans, K.K., Horowitz, T.S., and Wolfe, J.M. "Auditory and Visual Memory in Musicians and Nonmusicians', in *Psychonomic Bulletin & Review* 18(3), 2011, 586–591. pmid:21374094

Conti, G. "Tempus Fugit: Four Strategies to Maximise MFL Curriculum Time", *The Language Gym*, 2017, available at https://gianfrancoconti.com/2017/07/29/tempus-fugit-irreparabile-four-strategies-to-maximise-your-curriculum-time/ (accessed 30.12.2019)

Counsell, C. "History" in A. Standish and A. Cuthbert, (Eds.), *What Should Schools Teach?* pp. 73–87. London: UCL Institute of Education Press, 2017

Counsell, C. "Better Conversations with Subject Leaders" in Sealy, C. (Ed.) *The researchED Guide to the Curriculum*, pp. 95–121. Woodbridge: John Catt, 2020

Davies, B. *Drawing on the Right Side of the Brain.* Los Angeles: JP Tarcher, 1994

Dawkins, R. *The Extended Phenotype.* Oxford: Oxford University Press, 1982

The Department for Education. The National Curriculum in England: Framework Document, 2014, available at https://assets.publishing.service.gov.uk/government/uploads/system/uploads/attachment_data/file/381344/Master_final_national_curriculum_28_Nov.pdf (accessed 1.08.2020)

Didau, D. *Making Meaning in English.* Abingdon: Routledge, 2021

Enser, M. *Making Every Geography Lesson Count.* Carmarthen: Crown House, 2019

Fairclough, N. *Language and Power.* Harlow: Pearson, 1989

Foster, R. "On Weaving an English Curriculum", *The Learning Profession*, 2020; available at https://thelearningprofession.com/2020/07/30/weaving-an-english-curriculum/ (accessed 1.08.2020)

Geary, D. "Principles of Evolutionary Educational Psychology" in *Learning and Individual Differences* Vol. 12, 317–325, 2013

Husbands, C. *What is History Teaching?* Buckingham: Open University Press, 1996

Kueh, R. "A Matter of Discipline? Knowledge, Curriculum and the Disciplinary in RE" in *RE Today* 37 (1), 55–59, 2019

Lidwell, W., Holden, K. and Butler, J. *Universal Principles of Design.* Beverly, MA: Rockport, 2010

Lightbrown, P. *How Languages are Learned.* Oxford: Oxford University Press, 2006

Maude, A. "What Might Powerful Geographical Knowledge Look Like?" In *Geography* 101, 70-76, 2016

Maxwell, J. *Making Every MFL Lesson Count.* Carmarthen: Crown House, 2019

McCourt, M. *Teaching for Mastery.* Woodbridge: John Catt, 2019

Needham, T. "The 6 Skills: An Overview and Skill 1: Tentative Language", Tom Needham Teach, 2019, available at https://tomneedhamteach.wordpress.com/2019/03/18/the-6-skills-an-overview-and-skill-1-tentative-language/ (accessed 27.12.2019)

Norman, E., Cubbitt, J., Urry, S. and Whittaker, M. *Advanced Design and Technology*, (3rd ed.). Harlow: Pearson, 2000

Oldfield, S., et al. Norfolk Agreed Syllabus, 2019 available at https://www.schools.norfolk.gov.uk/-/media/schools/files/teaching-and-learning/religious-education-agreed-syllabus/norfolk-religious-education-agreed-syllabus-2019.pdf (accessed 15.05.20)

Pinker, S. *The Language Instinct.* London: Penguin, 1994

Riley, M. "Into the Key Stage Three History Garden: Choosing and Planting your Enquiry Questions" in *Teaching History* 99, 8–13, 2008

Scruton, R. *The Soul of the World.* Oxford: Princeton University Press, 2014

Smith, A. "Teaching Beautifully: The Best of What Has Been Drawn and Seen", Mr Smith RE, 2019, available at https://mrsmithre.home.blog/2019/11/09/teaching-beautifully-the-best-of-what-has-been-drawn-and-seen/ (accessed 31.12.19)

Sturdy, G. "Physics" in A. Standish, and A. Cuthbert, *What Should Schools Teach?* London: UCL Institute of Education Press, 2017

Titon, J. *Worlds of Music: An Introduction to the Music of the World's Peoples*, (5th ed.). Belmont, CA: Schirmer Cengage Learning, 2009

Vorderman, C. *Help Your Kids With Music.* London: Dorling Kindersley, 2015

Walter, C. "Mapping Skills Across Key Stage Three", Educaiti, 2020, available at https://educaiti.com/blog/mapping-skills-across-key-stage-3 (accessed 4.08.2020)

Waugh, D. *Geography: An Integrated Approach.* Cheltenham: Nelson Thornes, 2000

Willingham, D. *Why Don't Students Like School.* San Francisco: Jossey Bass, 2010

Wing, J. "Computational Thinking", Microsoft Research Asia Faculty Summit, 2012, available at https://www.microsoft.com/en-us/research/wp-content/uploads/2012/08/Jeannette_Wing.pdf (accessed 2.01.2020)

Woodcock, J. "Does the Linguistic Release the Conceptual" in *Teaching History*, 119, 5–14, 2005

Wrangham, R. *Catching Fire.* London: Profile, 2009

5 THE CODIFICATION OF CURRICULUM

An introduction to codification

The substance of what is taught – the content, in all its details, themes, ideas and processes[1] – and its mapping over time, are the objects of curriculum work, and the material of these objects must be fed largely by the subject discourse as has been described in Section 2.3. The *work* to be undertaken by students, in questions, tasks, exercises, practice and the like, can also be understood as a key constituent of curriculum, since it directly reflects the content to be learned, and the route towards greater mastery of subject specialism.

The specifics of curriculum planning across both taught content and its associated *work*, in both the big picture and the lesson-to-lesson detail, are almost exclusively subject-specific and can only be informed in a most general sense by the ideas in this book. Most of the development will need to be led by careful thought about, and engagement with, the subject and its discourse, the detail of the content and the ways that children learn in relation to these specifics.

In codifying – i.e. in writing down – the content and student work of curriculum into maps, booklets and other working documents, we find a powerful lever in the development of both curriculum and teachers. Through codification we can free up teachers to spend time on subject knowledge and pedagogy planning, rather than producing or searching for resources; we can provide, too, a minimum guarantee of content and practice for all students. For these reasons, the codification of curriculum is a crucial component of curriculum work.

In this section we explore the opportunities for, and benefits of, the codification of content and student practice. A critical theme will be that the documents themselves are only the smallest part of the success of codification; it is the planned discussion and professional development around these documents, and what is done with them once they have been produced, that results in deep and sustained growth within a department.

5.1 The value of codification

Why codify? Writing things down forces the writer to think. No one has ever explored all the knowledge, links, progressions, examples, and scholarship in their subject, and no-one ever will, for these things are not only vast, they are continually added to and ever altered and refined by those working in the fields of production and recontextualisation (see Section 3.1). Mapping things out on a document is an aid to thought; great minds have outsourced their mental capacity in this way throughout history, and doing so is an invaluable tool to the curriculum thinker.[2]

Having curricular plans laid out on a document that can be seen and pointed at facilitates both sharing and development. It is the job of the leader of a department to develop their team's understanding to a level where everyone can see the progression designed into the whole curriculum; where they know what knowledge is being built on now and which will be built on later; which details to draw out and why; what must be mastered and retained, and what serves as illustration or hinterland rather than as core knowledge. If subject leaders can point at all of these things while they discuss curriculum, and others can do the same – if they can ask questions, make clarifications, and reach out into the understanding that is made concrete in the document – then there obtains a powerful sharing of meaning and a vehicle for building engagement with the curriculum thinking in the department. Conversations outside of the department, for example within the senior leadership team (SLT), are similarly supported by these documents; sharing in a visible representation is a potent tool for sharing vision.

For the detail of curriculum, the codification into booklets or some other format serves several crucial purposes. Having the majority of the intended content, examples, and practice planned and laid out in a document is an important lever for ensuring the intended content makes its way into lessons. When staff are using such tools there is no more individual choice in the lesson-planning stage over *what* students are taught. This is not to say that teachers should not have input into this, but that such input cannot be left to happen at the point of individual planning.

There are good reasons why such decision making should not be left to individuals.

1. Quality-assuring curricular decisions is not practicable at the point of individual lesson planning.

2. Leaving curriculum to chance in this way sets children up to have gaps, jolts, and disconnects in their education over the years, as they experience the preferences of one teacher in one year and another in the subsequent year.

3. Content easily drifts into incoherence over the long term. Indeed, the level of thinking that must go into planning a genuinely coherent and rich curriculum is enormous, and to imply that that thinking should be carried out as many times as there are teachers in a department is a wildly unrealistic approach to those most precious of resources, time and intellect.

It must be for department leaders to lead and coordinate their department's input into curriculum planning so that the diet children receive is consistently good, and that the unfolding of narrative and building of knowledge across the years is systematic and meaningful. It is by no means the case that curriculum must always be written by a single department leader (in fact, this should, where possible, be avoided) but that collaborative work must be planned centrally. Decisions must be made and assured long before they make it into teachers' planning and the lessons themselves. This allows individual teachers to focus their planning on the specific adaptation of the material and its delivery for the students in their classes.

In a codified curriculum document, such as a booklet of reading, resources, model answers and practice questions, we can include carefully chosen and written explanations, examples, modelling and practice, and these should be available to all students, regardless of their teacher. The resources for teaching a great lesson should be available to all staff; no-one should be scrabbling around either trying to create, find, or photocopy resources at the last moment. Booklets and other codification documents simplify everything and free teachers to concentrate on routines, modelling, questioning, and subject knowledge. Teachers' time, as we have noted, must be treasured; codification can significantly improve how this limited resource is used.

The pedagogical benefits of documents such as booklets can be extraordinary. For one thing, through their use students are routinely required to read academic text, something which is otherwise often missing from a great many lessons. Students can work through questions at a rapid pace, and a great many questions can be set, allowing ambitious and flexible working in lessons. In schools where booklets are used well, students' work is truly remarkable.[3]

The writing or editing of curriculum booklets or similar codification can in itself be powerful professional development for teachers. The amount of research, thinking and reflection that should be put into the production of these documents is a highly valuable professional development undertaking. It must be remembered here though that within a department, booklets and the like will necessarily be used by staff other than the authors. This is desirable, for workload, standardisation, and the benefits of exploring another's work – but there are dangers too. If booklets or other codified curriculum resources are treated as "pick-up-and-go", then teaching can suffer considerably. A well-prepared teacher will have read, considered, and explored the whole document – as well as having understood the detail of the curriculum mapping – in order to be sure of understanding the knowledge, the answers to questions posed, and the relationship of the knowledge in this component of a curriculum to that contained within the bigger picture.

The well-prepared teacher will be able to confidently model or explain the work in a booklet and equivalent additional examples or related details. They will also be able to answer student questions not directly covered in the booklet. None of this is a given – such preparedness results only from thorough planning and subject knowledge development. Using department time to discuss codification documents and their use (see Section 2.3) is an effective way not only of developing teachers' curricular understanding, but also of modelling the required preparation for using these documents and of beginning to build those habits of planning that lead to effective enactment in the classroom.

Once a department reaches a point of codification for all units for all years, it would be a mistake to think that their work is done. Codification represents a huge step forward but it is really just a part of a beginning of a new era of curriculum culture. A continuous cycle of iteration and reflection, of pointing at documents and debating, of feeding thought with reading and engagement with the subject discourse; all of these are characteristic of a department with an excellent relationship to the curriculum.

5.2 Some explorations of codification

Let us now consider some of the material that can be usefully codified in curriculum work.

5.2.1 Knowledge analysis and explicit structure

Success in any subject depends on the remembering, bringing-together, and application of a broad range of components. It should be understood that many of these components may at first be invisible to teachers, who suffer from "the curse of knowledge",[4] where an expert does not recognise all of the knowledge she has internalised, and fails to make it explicit to others as a result. The components of knowledge in a subject can be grouped into different types of knowledge, or strands, such as declarative and procedural, or substantive and disciplinary (see Section 3.3) and relate across several planes of meaning (see Section 3.4). Mapping out the areas of knowledge, grouping components for meaning on a page or screen, is a valuable form of codification, making the implicit explicit and allowing deep thought and discussion. Consider Figure 5.1, taken from the subject section on "Design and technology".

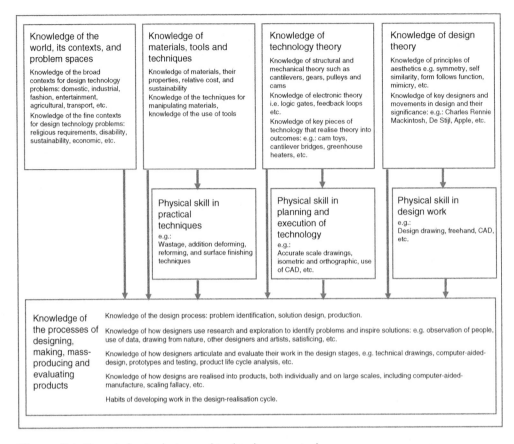

Figure 5.1 Knowledge in design and technology curriculum

To be able to think of the knowledge in design technology using these categories allows several important things to happen. It supports the naming of the things that must be learned, the components of excellence, and therefore the explicit inclusion and development of these throughout the planned curriculum. Without this itemisation it is easy to view curriculum in design and technology as a disconnected series of projects, with much knowledge left implicit. These categories allow us to ask how we can be more ambitious for students and construct an increasingly powerful curriculum, rich with sophistication in the theory and techniques of each of the strands.

The components of knowledge in a subject do not exist in isolation from each other. They are linked, and these links are important: they are the highways of thought. Drawing out these links is another valuable process for clarifying thinking and revealing the hidden features of expertise. The act of codifying forces us to make explicit the strands of curriculum components and the links between them. Although this thinking, the discourse around it, and the codification of that thought in a diagram or other format, takes time, such time is a worthwhile investment. Investing this time builds deep foundations for curriculum work and allows a strong structure of sequence, progression, and meaning to be built across the curriculum both as a whole and from one lesson to another.

To return to our example from design technology, the links between the strands indicate ways in which curriculum might be structured. A project might, for example, begin with studying some contexts in the field, and the work of some key designers such as Gerrit Rietveld, or Charles and Ray Eames, explicating some of the design theory manifest in their work such as abstraction, the banana leaf parable, and negative space. There might then follow some work on materials such as woods, and the techniques for their use in design work. Practical instruction in both design drawing and execution could then feed into a quasi-project, where students are shown and emulate the stages of project development in design technology work. While the sequencing here may be fairly intuitive, the work of the details and ambition of each stage, and their relation to other details is strongly supported in the mapping and linking of the knowledge strands as above. These details might be codified through a combination of printed booklets with written, photographic, and diagrammatic explications, physical artefacts, and either detailed notes, modelling through department meetings, or video recordings of the level of explanation to be given through teacher demonstration.

In Section 3.3 we explored some approaches to understanding types of knowledge found in the subjects. Chapter 4 included some suggested broad knowledge analyses and structures to give insight into the subjects. The ideas in these sections may be useful as starting points for departments developing their own codification. While it is not important for subject leaders to use a particular lexicon to describe the components, differences, and structures of knowledge within their subject, where there is agreed language within the subject community it is wise to assimilate it. What is most important is that these ideas and relationships are thought about and laid out on paper. Codification of knowledge in types and relations are key in promoting thought, powerful and ambitious curriculum planning, and the alignment of all members of a department in this understanding.

5.2.2 Progression models

In Section 3.5 we explored the theory of progression, particularly the question of what it means to get better at a subject. This question is one that must be answered in order to plan effective curriculum and indeed assessment, but it is one that is initially difficult to answer. We can begin by pointing at knowledge analyses and maps such as those discussed above, and being clear that progression means, "getting better at each of these things." (Figure 5.2)

From this, two more questions follow:

▓ What does success "look like;" what are the components of success in each of these things?

▓ What teaching activities and exercises can support students to get better at these things?

Statement of Model of Progression

Substantive knowledge - the facts and content

1. More facts, e.g. the charge on the electron is -1
2. More explanations, e.g. ionic compounds have high melting points because...
3. More links between facts, e.g. electrons cause static and current electricity and chemical properties
4. Recognise more scenarios as being instances of principles and apply those principles to answer the questions
5. Use more subject specialist terminology in explanations

Disciplinary knowledge - knowledge of how this discipline works

1. Plan increasingly sophisticated investigations (awareness that these are contingent on the substantive knowledge)
2. More procedures, e.g. drawing dot and cross diagrams
3. Solve more multi-stage/ multi-part problems
4. Interpret increasingly complex experimental designs
5. Interpret increasingly complex data
6. Present data with increasing sophistication
7. Describe, with increasing levels of sophistication, the role of peer review, the relationship between theory and evidence, and the judgment of risk
8. Carry out all of the above in relation to an increasing field of substantive knowledge.
9. Write in an increasingly academic (scientific) register

Figure 5.2 A progression model for science curriculum

The resultant lists are a set of curricular content, and to sequence them in an appropriate order gives us a starting point for sequencing in the subject. Such codified models are useful both for those planning the grand sequencing and the detail of curriculum, and also for helping a team to understand the logic and structure of the planned curriculum, so that they can ensure the explicit manifestation of this progression within their teaching. These progression models are also key in assessment design, where we must ask two further questions:

- What should students be getting better at?

- How can we measure students' performance to check their progress?

5.2.3 Sequence and mapping

A codified map of the content to be taught over time across a curriculum is a powerful thing to have (Figure 5.3).

Seeing the place of each section of curriculum in relation to the finished whole allows staff to locate their current unit of teaching and understand its relation to

Week	Teaching	Substantive knowledge headlines	Disciplinary knowledge (HSW) headlines	Maths	Requisite knowledge from previous units	Links to knowledge in future units	Links to knowledge in previous units
1	Chem fundamentals						
2	Chem fundamentals			Calculating percentages (for percentage isotopes of compounds)			
3	Chem fundamentals	Structure of the atom, isotopes, ions, moles, periodic table	Using models to represent the unobservable		KS2: solids, liquids and gases	Foreshadowing of bonding	
4	Chem fundamentals						
5	HSW: Investigation						
6	HSW: Investigation	How does the reactivity of group 2 elements change as you go down the group?	Planning, carrying out, and interpreting an investigation	Bar charts of results	Properties of matter and chemical reactions	(All future investigations and related truth-claims)	Chem fundamentals
7	HSW: Investigation						
8	Radioactivity						
9	Radioactivity	Alpha beta and gamma composition and properties, hazards of radiation	Reading from graphs	Percentages	Subatomic particles and their properties, periodic table, ions	Forces	Atomic structure, periodic table
10	Radioactivity						
11	HSW: Science in society: Risk and peer review		The types of questions science can and can't answer; peer review; evaluating risk		Radioactivity, ions, atoms,		Radioactivity, ions
12	HSW: Science in society: Risk and peer review						
13	Four fundamental forces						
14	Four fundamental forces	Definition of forces, Newton 3, gravity, electrostatic and magnetism	Planning, carrying out, and interpreting an investigation	Units, Multiplication and Division	KS2: Forces; Subatomic particles	Resolving forces; Newton 1 and 2	Atomic structure
15	Four fundamental forces						

Figure 5.3 A section of a curriculum sequence map for science (KS3)

the rest of the curriculum. This is key to the shared curricular understanding in a department. Being able to point to this document and discuss it as a team is a mechanism for developing that shared understanding and facilitates such discussions as:

- Why this, why now?"[5]

- What are the links between knowledge?

- What are the sequencing principles for teaching different areas of the curriculum? (Section 3.6)

- What is the detail of the content and its development over time?

- What would happen if we did this here instead of there?

- How should we accommodate ideas brought in from wider subject discourse?

In mapping or sequencing documents, it is also useful to include details such as:

- the components and strands

- progression points

- links to past and future content

- prerequisite knowledge for components.

These details serve several purposes. Their inclusion in the mapping forces careful thought and often adaptations to the mapping as critical points are brought to light. The discussion of these details within a team can make for excellent professional subject development. Being able to refer to a document making all of these things explicit empowers classroom teachers to ensure these ingredients are explicit in individual planning and lessons. In addition, codified documents facilitate the planning of assessment for learning prerequisite knowledge, preparing for student questions, and looking both forward and back in the curriculum.

5.2.4 Lesson resources and booklets

Finally, we come to the codification of lesson content, in booklets or some other medium. Figure 5.4 gives us an example of a page from a booklet used in English. These documents have immense value in:

- guaranteeing the content of taught lessons

- providing a strong starting point for staff planning

- prompting curriculum discussions as professional development.

Let us consider some of the components that are typical of these documents.

Act 1, scene 2: Summary

At a military camp near his palace at Forres, King Duncan of Scotland asks a wounded captain for news about the Scots' battle with the Irish invaders, who are led by the rebel Macdonald. The captain, who was wounded helping Duncan's son Malcolm escape capture by the Irish, replies that the Scottish generals Macbeth and Banquo fought with great courage and violence. The captain then describes for Duncan how Macbeth killed the traitorous Macdonald. As the captain is carried off to have his wounds attended to, the thane of Ross, a Scottish nobleman, enters and tells the king that the traitorous **_thane_** of Cawdor has been defeated and the army of Norway repelled. Duncan decrees that the thane of Cawdor be put to death and that Macbeth, the hero of the victorious army, be given Cawdor's title. Ross leaves to deliver the news to Macbeth.

Thane	A Scottish Lord

Questions:
1) Who are the Scots fighting?
2) Who is the leader of the rebels?
3) How did Banquo and Macbeth fight?
4) What did Macbeth do to Macdonald?
5) What does the Thane of Ross tell the King?
6) What is Macbeth given and why?

Act 1 Scene 2: Vocabulary

laud (v)	praise (a person or their achievements) highly
	Macbeth's actions in battle are lauded by the Captain who calls him 'brave'.
Ruthless (adj)	Having or showing no pity
Ruthlessness (n)	*Macbeth is a ruthless warrior who 'carved out his passage' through the enemy*
Brutal (adj)	Savagely violent
Brutality (n)	*Macbeth 'unseamed him from the knave to the chaps', a brutal and vicious attack.*
Valiant (adj)	possessing or showing courage or determination
	A valiant warrior, Macbeth fought 'like valour's minion'
Relentless (adj)	unceasingly intense, never ending
Relentlessness (n)	*Relentless and brutal, Macbeth fought so hard that his 'brandished steel…smoked with bloody execution'*
Venerate (v)	regard with great respect; revere.
veneration (n)	*Venerated by Duncan who calls him 'noble', Macbeth is universally lauded at the beginning of the play.*

How is Macbeth Presented in Act 1 Scene 2?

Model Paragraph: Macbeth has been fighting for King Duncan and defending Scotland against an invasion, led by the rebel, Macdonald. A Captain lauds Macbeth's actions in battle, calling him 'brave' and adding that he 'deserves that name' as if there is no doubt that Macbeth is a fearless warrior who is committed to protecting his King and country. Macbeth is so determined and loyal that he was

5 'disdaining fortune' as if he didn't care about fate, luck or the risk involved in battle, further evidence that he is valiant. He had a 'brandished steel', an image that hints at pride and power. Relentless and brutal, Macbeth fought so hard that his 'brandished steel…smoked with bloody execution'. A ruthless warrior, Macbeth 'carved out his passage' through the enemy, another violent and graphic image that presents Macbeth's skill and devotion in battle. Macbeth's violence here is not just acceptable, but is

10 explicitly venerated, and he uses it to serve his King. Described as 'valour's minion', he is valiant, loyal and fearless. The word 'minion' suggests that Macbeth is utterly committed to the ideas of bravery and courage. It is as if bravery is his master and he serves it without question.

Figure 5.4 A page from an English booklet on Macbeth[8]

An excellent starting point for comprehensive lesson codification is an explication of lesson content, such as written material of the content it is desired that students encounter. This explication should:

- reflect the detail and ambition begun in the knowledge analysis, progression models, and sequencing work described above

- make use of principles of excellence in explanation (such as those laid out in the cognitive science/explicit instruction literature[6])

- reflect thinking fed by the field of the subject discourse.[7]

The codification of work for students (questions, tasks, activities and so on) will also be key to these materials. It is in the carrying out of work that students are able to build their own understanding, and this building is as critical as the intended content itself. As far as possible, this must not be left underdetermined.

Again, there is a great deal of theory that may be applied here in order to design highly effective work and the sequencing thereof. Worked and faded examples,[9] analysis of scholarship, atomisation of processes and sentence-level tasks[10] are all examples from teaching theory that can contribute to effective booklet or other lesson material design.

The modelling of excellence in codified documents is a highly valuable inclusion, though such exemplar material must be understood as a complement to, not as a replacement for, live modelling in the classroom. Worked solutions to problems, and exemplar pieces of writing, are two examples here, though it is important with this latter that the exemplars really do demonstrate excellence, and are not just sufficient for "top marks". Thinking in terms of grades and assessment objectives can often undermine the ambition of the material modelled for students. In many subjects, scholarship from the field of production is a meaningful inclusion in booklets or other codifications. Writing from renowned scholars can serve not only as a vehicle for content and a starting point for discussions, but as exemplar material in itself, amenable to taught analysis and structured emulation in practice.

A common thread through much of the codification of lesson content is that of student engagement in reading. The quality of the material read by students – and that read to them in lessons – has great influence over their experience of curriculum and their development as both readers and writers. The inclusion of scholarship is an obvious lever for elevating the quality of what students read, but the quality of the text throughout lesson resources is also key. Where homegrown text is ambitious and well-written, with academic vocabulary and varied and effective sentence structures, the student experience is greatly enhanced. This work is fed by reading, practice, and feedback from other specialists and leaders, and must not be underestimated in its importance.

5.2.5 Access

While it is the case that some students join secondary school unable to access these sorts of texts, this must be interpreted as a need for effective reading intervention so that students are rapidly brought to a level where they can access these materials, rather than a reason to lower curricular expectations for those students. It is also the case that some students will master some content more quickly than others, and this may at first look more difficult to reconcile with an ambition for all students. What should we do about the fact that some children will sometimes take longer to learn some things than others? We can use effective teaching practices such as explicit instruction and retrieval practice, and well-designed curriculum to ensure that even those who learn the least still learn an impressive amount. We can be clear in our curriculum planning about what must be secure, and make use of assessment for learning to ensure that such "golden knowledge" has been mastered before moving on. And crucially, we can rely only on this assessment for learning, rather than prior attainment, target grades, or any other mispurposed data item, to make these decisions on a case-by-case, piece-by-piece basis.

5.3 Codification in a state of flux

A fully codified curriculum, with the documents described in this section, supports careful planning of curriculum, allows effective staff development, and frees up teacher planning time for lesson delivery and responsive teaching. It is a mistake, however, to view a fully codified curriculum as an end-point after which work on codification should stop. Curriculum thinking is a never-ending process, since there is always more to think about, and always new discourse to respond to, and these developments in thinking must feed into an ever-developing codified curriculum. The involvement of staff, over time, in the discussion and development of codified curriculum is key to the development of both the curriculum and staff, and is a crucial component in a strong culture of curriculum and commitment to continuous improvement. This involvement takes time and must be explicitly planned for but is indispensable in the long term. Not only does this approach develop both individual staff and collective departmental thinking, it also reflects the true nature of knowledge and curriculum as constructs with essential ongoing developments and debates, nurturing an authentic epistemological approach root-and-branch throughout the department.

5.4 Questions for discussion

▦ What codification should be developed for this subject?

▦ What sources can be drawn on to inform this codification?

▦ What should be the characteristics of the input/content?

▦ What should be the characteristics of the work/practice?

▦ How should codification reflect thinking on the components of curriculum (described in Chapters 6–12)?

▦ How should codification be used for staff development?

▦ How can the engagement of staff with codification and the ideas behind it be explored?

Notes

1 It is important to remember that these categories denote different types of thing, and do different work, in different subjects.
2 Socrates didn't, but then, the only reason we know about him is because Plato did. See Plato's *Phraedrus*.
3 See the work of the West London Free School, Michaela Community School, and the Bedford Free School, among others
4 Heath and Heath (2006)
5 Turner (2018)
6 See e. g. Tharby (2018) and Engelmann and Carnine (1982)
7 See e.g. https://www.history.org.uk/publications/categories/teaching-history and https://cogscisci.wordpress.com/
8 Needham (2020)
9 See e.g. Needham (2020)
10 See e.g. Hochman and Wexler (2017)

References

Engelmann, S. and Carnine, D. *Theory of Instruction*. New York: Irvington, 1982
Heath, C. and Heath, D. "The Curse of Knowledge" in *Harvard Business Review*, 2006, available at: https://hbr.org/2006/12/the-curse-of-knowledge (accessed 13.02.2020)
Hochman, J. and Wexler, N. *The Writing Revolution*. San Francisco: Jossey-Bass, 2017
Needham, T., Macbeth Booklet Part 1, 2020 (unpublished)
Tharby, A. *How to Explain Absolutely Anything to Anyone*. Carmarthen: Crown House, 2018
Turner, S. "Developing Your Curriculum Design Skills", in *Impact*, 4, June 2018, available at: https://impact.chartered.college/article/turner-developing-your-curriculum-design-skills/ (accessed 18.02.2021)

Conclusion

The thirteen school subjects explored thus far represent some of the most significant, uplifting, transcendental and moving bodies of knowledge and culture that have been achieved by our species in our time on this Earth, and if time and space were no object there are probably thirteen more worthy of the same exploration. There is undoubtedly a diversity of ways of representing and understanding the knowledge in the subjects, and it is hoped that those presented here may be starting points for much deeper analysis and discussion.

Michael Young's conception of Powerful Knowledge and Future 3 give us an inescapable moral imperative for seeking ambitious curriculum in the subject specialisms. The power of knowledge – to lift us beyond the everyday, to make meaning from the world, and to feed healthy democracy – is plain to see. To begin to gaze upon our subjects as we have, in all their glittering colours, to uncover their structures, and to take up the mantles of their quests – all of this makes that imperative seem all the more urgent. The knowledge held and renewed in the disciplines is a wonderful and precious gift; to be custodians and passers-on of that knowledge through our work in schools is at once a great privilege and grave responsibility.

The relations of curriculum to mind and memory are complicated, but models from cognitive science can not only show us that ambitious curriculum can be accessed by all, but that also begin to provide cognitive foundations for elements of curriculum thinking, such as types of knowledge, sequencing, interweaving, and retrieval.

A culture of intellectualism is essential for rich and sustained curriculum work, and this is something that can be intentionally planned for and built. The codification of curriculum is a powerful tool for giving shape to thinking and shared meaning for staff development. Ongoing engagement with the subject discourse is an essential factor in curriculum work of quality.

In order to steer and lead culture and subject engagement of this kind, senior leaders must have a firm grasp of cognitive models for teaching, and of general curriculum theory. We must feel the urgency of the moral imperative, and we must have authentic, if necessarily limited, understanding and appreciation of the subjects: their natures, structures, the type of meaning they make from the world, and how they make that meaning. These understandings can only ever be starting points, questions for discussion, pointers for engagement with other specialists. The temptation for reduction must be resisted and a lasting and growing discourse built over time. Knowledge of the limitations of our knowledge sets schools free from genericism and weak thinking, since it liberates us to seek wisdom in the wider specialist conversation. Such leadership takes courage, long hours of reading and asking many, many questions, but the fruits of curriculum are sweet and the roots, while they may be hard work, are not so bitter.

Acknowledgements

I am indebted to the following people for the insights they have given me either in my reading of their work, in passing conversation, deep discussion, or in looking over various drafts of this work and offering their feedback. For your time, wisdom, and patience, I thank you.

David Didau
Dave Edwards
Steve Lane
Dawn Cox
Sarah Barker
Amy Forrester
Rebecca Foster
Ben Ranson
Mark Enser
Matt Burnage
Tim Jenner
Johnathan Stephens
Adam Boxer
Adam Robbins
Chris Baker
Matthew Benyohai
Gary Davies
Bill Wilkinson
Antonia Blanchflower
Clare Sealy
Christine Counsell
Sam Hall
Tom Needham
Martin Robinson
Pritesh Raichura
Gareth Sturdy

Mark McCourt
Bob Pritchard
Gethyn Jones
Deep Ghataura
Tom Millichamp
Louisa Aron
Grainne Hallahan
Andrew Percival
Grace Healy
Dan Green
Tom Ashbee
Alan Harrison
Christian Moore Anderson
Ed Clarke
John Bald
Adam Smith
Richard Kueh
Jim Carroll
Jemma Sherwood
Daisy Christodoulou
Mark Lehain
Atlanta Plowden
Michael Young
Sue Gerrard
Helen Georgiou
Karl Maton
Kev Llewellyn
Jonathan Caslake
Annamarie Kino
Katharine Bartlett
Molly Selby
Saritha Srinivasan

Glossary

analysis-reduction creep The problem arising where one mistakes the utility of analysis in the form of lists, categories and so on, to be a complete representation of the nature of the domain in question, and the holistic or emergent properties of a domain are lost through an erroneous pursuit of lists etc. as an end in themselves

approval The methods through which knowledge or meaning are agreed to form part of the body of established material in a discipline

being-in-the-world (*dasein*) Heidegger's concept of human existence as an engagement with the world in some way

booklet A paper booklet containing written or drawn knowledge and questions or other work for students to undertake in lessons. May contain other materials such as glossaries, examples of scholarship, or maps relating the topic to the wider subject, for example

chunking The cognitive process of linking pieces of information together into larger units by virtue of a shared meaning or association

codification The process, and results, of writing down and/or drawing out ideas in curriculum work, including areas of knowledge, sequences, the details of what is taught and the work that will be undertaken by students

collective sufficiency The property of a group of things, such as pieces of knowledge, where together they furnish sufficient understanding, although individually none can be said to be essential

core The headline knowledge, that which remains explicit in long-term memory

curricular objects Ideas, processes, or other items that are part of the intended learning as a result of a curriculum

curriculum The substance of what is taught, structured over time

declarative knowledge Knowledge of propositions

disciplinary code The rules and conventions, often unspoken, by which a discipline or field operates

disciplinary knowledge Knowledge of how a discipline generates knowledge or meaning in the world

discipline Both a body of knowledge and the associated institutions and specialists, typified by, among other things, departments in higher education, a specialist body of terminology and concepts, systems for approval of work within the discipline, and a specialist way of viewing the world

discourse The body of conversations, both past and ongoing, in a given domain. Typically manifest in a variety of media including books, journals, and social media

epistemological To do with how knowledge is acquired

epistemological patterns The patterns in which new knowledge or meaning is approved within a discipline; typically either unifying or discursive or accumulative

field of production The area where new knowledge or meaning is generated: universities, industries, and individuals

field of recontextualisation The area where knowledge from the field of production is selected and reformatted for teaching in educational settings. Examples of the field of recontextualisation are examination boards, government education departments, and textbook publishing houses

field of reproduction The area in which students begin their education in a subject; typically schools, home-schooling and tutoring

gaze A particular outlook or way of looking at the world

genericism The approach of forcing generic models or practices on very different areas, leading to distortions and weak thinking

hinterland The background knowledge that furnishes richness and depth, and may later serve important core knowledge as it is brought to the fore

independent necessity Of a piece of knowledge, the property of it being, on its own, necessary for progression

integration of knowledge Of relations between knowledge in a domain, a measure of how tightly defined and agreed such relations are

interweaving The process, in curriculum design, of planning the explicit teaching of links across disparate parts of the domain

knower The student, specialist, or other participant in knowledge in a given domain

Knowledge-analysis document A codification in which the types of knowledge within a curriculum are identified, with details of the sorts of knowledge included

Lebenswelt Husserl's conception of the "life-world" – a shared world in which individuals meet in their shared experience

living-in From Polanyi's *indwelling* – the conception of a knower's experience of knowledge as an extension of the self

manthanology A property of knowledge, articulating the level of dependency of knowledge on other previously learned knowledge

meaning A property of a knower's relation with knowledge, where significance beyond the surface-level is experienced by the knower

narrative   The story-like properties of a curriculum

ontological   To do with the objects of a discipline or subject

ontological architecture   The relationships between the objects of interest in a discipline or subject

powerful knowledge   Young's conception of knowledge that takes us beyond the everyday, and describes both the objects of a discipline and its ways of working

procedural knowledge   Knowledge of processes

progression   The property of knowledge in curriculum developing in a meaningful way

quest   The purpose, orientation, or drive of a discipline

recontextualisation   The process of selecting and adapting knowledge from the field of production in order to create appropriate curriculum for the field of reproduction

renewal   The process of carrying out a subject in a disciplinary sense, often in classrooms, and making meaning for the learners although not producing new knowledge or meaning in the sense we have in the field of production

semantic density   From Legitimation Code Theory, the property of knowledge describing the extent to which areas in the domain are linked to one another

semantic gravity   From Legitimation Code Theory, the property of knowledge describing the extent to which knowledge is tied to context

semantic waving   From Legitimation Code Theory, the practice of moving from specific context, to more context-free principle, and then to another specific context

sequence   The order of material in curriculum

sequence document   A codification in which the order of material is laid out, with unit titles but also key knowledge headlines within the units, so that narrative and progression can be seen across the years

social realism   From sociology, an approach under which objectivist and rational knowledge is understood to be a social phenomenon

sociological   Relating to the behaviour of groups of people and/or institutions

subject community   The people involved in discourse around a subject, often both formally and informally, through organised groups and ad hoc exchanges

subjects   The recontextualised knowledge domains and their conventions found in schools

substantive knowledge   Knowledge of the claims about the world, or meaning put into the world, by a discipline

synthesis   The bringing-together of component parts

truth-status   The understandings given to the nature of truth-claims in a subject

Index

Page numbers in *italics* refer to figures and those in bold refer to tables.

Printed in Great Britain
by Amazon

82567863R00086